Through the Mists of Faerie:

A Magical Guide to the Wisdom Teachings
of the Ancient Elven

By The Silver Elves

Copyright © 2012 The Silver Elves, Michael J Love and Martha C. Love

All rights reserved.
Cover photo is of Syndaryn, our beloved elven daughter.

ISBN-13: 978-1480064973
ISBN-10: 1480064971
Printed in the United States of America by CreateSpace

Without limiting the rights under the copyright reserved above, no part of this publication may be reproduced, stored in or introduced into a retrieval system, or transmitted in any form or by any means (electronic, mechanical, by photocopying, recording or otherwise) without the prior written permission of the copyright owner and the publisher of the book.

DEDICATION

This book is dedicated to our sister Syleniel and our kindred of the Elenari.

> *"IF YOU LOOK TO OTHERS TO TELL YOU WHAT YOUR DREAMS SHOULD BE, YOU'LL WIND UP LIVING OTHER PEOPLE'S DREAMS."*
> —*OLD ELVEN SAYING*

TABLE OF CONTENTS

INTRODUCTION 13
A Word About Pronouns 13

Section One: The Nature of the True S'elf

THE RIGHT TO PURSUE ONE'S OWN PATH 17

Coming to the Path 25

The Will to Mastery 32

The Plan 36

A Few Words About the Dark Lodge 36

The Goals of Evolutionary Life 37

The Evolving Aspect of Will 39

The Seeming Conflict 40

Knowing the Plan 44

The Underlying Assumption 45

Meditation 47

The Wiccan Rede 49

Astrology 51

Elven Kin 52

Integration of our Natures 53

The Body 54

Feelings 54

Thoughts 55

Soul 56

Spirit 56

The Lessons of the Soul 57

Being and Non-Being 59

Conscious and Un-Conscious 61

Pure Awareness 61

The Witnesses 64

Soul Mates and Soul Bonds 66

Vegetarianism 70

The Rationalizing Mind 71

The Quest 72

The Courtship 77

The Dancers 79

The Ego 82

Defining the S'elf 83

Training the Dog 88

The Power of Reason 89

Understanding the Student...90

On With the Dance of Romance 92

One of Silver, One of Gold 93

Joining the Dance 95

Giving the Devil his Due 96

Seeing Beyond the World 96

The Great Spirit 98

The Great Soul..98

Section Two: The Elven Way

THE AWAKENING OF THE HIGHER INSTINCTS...103

Old Souls and Old Spirits 105

Trails and Tribulations..106

The Magician and the Mystic 109

Leaders and Followers 110

Elvenhome..111

Elfland 112

Serenity...114

Hope Springs Eternal..118

Why Do We Call Ours'elves Elves 120

Finding the Source 121

How Do We Know What Is True? 122

You Are Your Own Master 123

The Thousandth Elfae 125

Facts and Knowledge 125

Vibrational Understanding 128

Enchantment 130

Know Thys'elf 131

Agreeing to Agree 135

Parallel Worlds 137

Doubts 138

Out Of Our Minds 141

The Great Mystery 143

True Knowing 144

Calling To Faerie 146

Creating the Atmosphere 147

Dealing With the Gods 149

Why Good Girls Like Bad Boys 157

Magic Happens 159

Mayavirupa 160

Meeting Ones'elf 161

The Humanity of Gods 163

Over-Shadowing 165

Sexual Attraction 167

The Separation of Spirit and Matter 170

The World Is One 171

Contagious 172

Elven Blood 172

The Swing 175

Effortlessness 178

Magic Costs 181

Everything Furthers 182

Giving the Body Its Due 184

Pursue Excellence 185

Section Three: Ancient Futures

ANCIENT FUTURE 191

The Seven Pointed Star 191
    1. The Presence: 192

- 2. Focus: 193
- 3. Calm Composure: 194
- 4. Inner Understanding: 195
- 5. Openness: 196
- 6. Appreciation 197
- 7. Altruism 198

The Seven Great Obstructions **200**
- 1. False Sense of S'elf 202
- 2. False Notion of the Universe 204
- 3. False Relationship 205
- 4. False Separation of Spirit and Matter 207
- 5. Self-Referencing 210
- 6. False Fulfillment 212
- 7. False Ritual 214

Section Four: The Shining Ones

SOULLESS OR SOULFUL? 219

The Shining Ones 223

The Elite 228

ABOUT THE AUTHORS 231

> "THERE ARE NEVER ANY STRINGS ATTACHED WITH ELFIN,
>
> IT IS EVER A MATTER OF FREE WILL,
>
> IT IS ONLY WHEN THE CHOICE IS FREE THAT MAGIC IS TRULY BINDING."
>
> —THE SILVER ELVES

INTRODUCTION

This is a book about High Elven Magic. Not the magic of chants and spells and ceremonies, of which we've already written quite a bit, but of the Quest to become like those of our kindred who we call the Shining Ones and which most folks think of when they fantasize about what elves are, even when they deny that we are elven or that elves exist at all. They are, of course, wrong on all counts.

This is the Way. If you would enter Faerie, or Elfin as we often call it, this is the Path that leads there.

Enjoy!

A Word About Pronouns

The English language does not have a pronoun that covers both male and female in instances when it could be either. For instance, if we wrote, "The magician did the magic and then left his or her magic circle", this would be correct English, but this "his or her", or "his/her", seems cumbersome to us. Most people write, "The magician did the magic and then left their magic circle." This creates an incorrect correlation between singular and plural, but is common usage. We have instead settled upon the use of "hir" which combines his and her, and sHe or SHe that combines she and he as an alternative.

—The Silver Elves

> "We elfin follow the way of Nature. Ours is the path of least resistance, which is the law of Nature. Some might take that to mean that we are submissive or easily dominated, but in truth, it indicates that we assist all beings in their quest toward fulfillment, including the wicked whom we aid in their head long rush toward destruction, by redirecting their energy away from the innocent and toward their own selves."
> —The Silver Elves

Section One:

The Nature of the True S'elf

> "FOR MOST PEOPLE'S HISTORY IS THE STORY OF BATTLES AND WARS THEY'VE LOST AND WON AND THE HEROES THERE OF. FOR WE ELFIN, HISTORY IS THE TALE OF THE MUSIC WE'VE COMPOSED, THE LITERATURE WE'VE WRITTEN AND THE ART WE'VE CREATED, AND THE LOVERS WHO INSPIRED IT ALL."
> —THE SILVER ELVES

THE RIGHT TO PURSUE ONE'S OWN PATH

One of the first challenges a newly awakened Elfae (combining the words elf and fae/faerie and meant to indicate all kindred of Elven/Faerie kind) encounters is the individual's right to decide for hir (combining the pronouns his and her, and used when the individual may be either male or female) own s'elf, hir direction, path and course. There are myriads of religious groups and cults all demanding that the elf follow their (the religious group's) beliefs or doctrines, and certainly nearly every elf comes from a background of religious, scientific, and/or ethnic culture. It is often difficult therefore to assert one's sense of s'elf when confronted by those persons and forces that one has been trained since birth to honor as authorities.

Whether one has been raised Christian, Jewish, Atheist, or Agnostic or some other faith, deciding to follow one's own path, particularly when one is young and inexperienced, can often be difficult. And unless one has come to despise, for whatever reasons, the teachings of one's childhood and family, one often wants to cling to the past while moving forward into the future. And for the elves this is not a problem. We are not concerned by those who wish to be elves and Christian, however, in our experience some Christian sects would make this balance difficult for their part. Like Voudoun, we elves have no problem incorporating the teachings and images of Christianity or Buddhism, Judaism, or even Islam into our understanding of our world. (Note that in Virginia there is found a stone in the form of a cross that is called the Fairy Cross that is said to link Jesus and the Fairy Folk.) The

Universe is One, and all that is in it is related to Faerie either directly or indirectly in the view of those with the Faerie Sight.

Jews and Hebrews often have a different experience. Many hold their religion easily in their hearts, but most will never give up their culture. At the same time the links between the Judaic and Hebraic peoples and the ancient Scythian lords from whom many of the elven have descended genetically, and upon whom the legends of faerie are in part based, are strong and linked by ancient marriage (see Laurence Gardner's *Realms of the Ring Lords*). So, again, on the elven side certainly, and probably on the Judaic and Hebrew side as well, there is very little friction between our peoples; and we elves certainly have always been very well treated and nurtured by our Judaic/Hebraic kin. Although, moving toward the full embrace and the living of the elven path can be a challenge for some who were raised in that culture. It often offers worldly connections and success that we elves, as yet, cannot offer them. Plus, while the Judaic-Hebrew culture is despised by some, and has been often persecuted in the world, they are none-the-less acknowledged by the world, even by those who despise them, while our Elven culture is seen by most as a foolish fantasy at best.

Those raised Atheist and Agnostic have a different challenge and this challenge curiously confronts many modern religious types as well. This is the idea that elves as an existent people and culture, is unscientific. They have been taught that we don't exist, are utterly the product of fantasy and have a difficult time accepting the reality of our existence. They are called to make a leap of faith into the unknown and this can be very difficult for folk raised in this fashion. If the reality of faerie isn't proven, they find it difficult to believe in. This challenge is reinforced by the social scorn they will have to endure if they do make that leap.

However, most Elfae are awakened by others of our kind, and while some may have a difficulty with relinquishing their former culture, and some may have difficulty believing in ideas that they have been told all their lives are mere imagination and fantasy, those who have heard the call inwardly, and who have encountered one or more of our living kindred, fully manifesting in the world, have a hard time denying the truth of their heart and experience.

Alas, here there are also powerful influences that confront the budding Elfae. There are the ancient legends and the modern tales concerning our kind, and many of these are simply erroneous and while inspiring the Elfae's heart, tend to confuse hir mind with often foolish and irrelevant aspects that may have been good for creating conflict and interest or dynamic tension in a story, but are inadequate and obstructive when the Elfae confronts hir real life in the world.

At the same time, if the elf who awakens hir is very powerful, or part of a group of very potent elven witches, it can be difficult for the newly awakened not to come completely under the sway of these more experienced elves. However, while these may be more experienced elves, and their magic may be more potent and powerful, it does not always mean they are more spiritually evolved or without aspects of their own soul and personality that need development. Every elf needs to reserve in hir own heart and mind the right to think for hirs'elf, and base hir judgments on hir own sense of inner guidance and direction. While we Elfae are all traveling toward Elfin/Faerie, we are not all of us journeying on the same exact paths. There are many paths to Faerie and many realms in Elfin.

It should be noted that it takes tremendous courage to stand against one's heritage and upbringing, and in many ways even greater courage to assert one's individual understanding of the path to those who awakened one. And we should remember, particularly at the beginning of this spiritual journey into the Realms of Elfin, not all Elfae are ready to venture on their own. Many need that guidance, and even if those who are providing it are not entirely evolved or perfected in their own elven souls, if they are not totally leading us astray like a bunch of errant pixies, their guidance may be of great help to us. Yet each Elfae should know that in the course of time, sHe (combining the pronouns she and he in instances where the individual may be either female or male) may hear the Call of Elfin drawing hir in another direction and if sHe is ready, should have no hesitation in pursuing it. Yet one is wise to keep in mind that in pursuing one's own path into Elfin/Faerie that not everyone will be ready to follow that path, particularly if one is blazing new trails through the Mists, and it is unwise, as well as un-elven, to attempt to force anyone to do so. Each needs to be encouraged on hir own way, at the level she currently has achieved, and is currently comfortable pursuing.

And one should know as well that in treading the Path of the Elven that most folks at this time in the world, mostly probably including one's oldest and closest friends, may be uncomfortable with this venture into the unknown. Your old friends like you as you are, and are often uncomfortable with you making what seems to them to be radical changes in your life. One thus may wish to be cautious in revealing one's elven nature to others. Most will simply ridicule the idea. Some, because of fundamentalist beliefs may be intimidated by the idea of magic and warn you against pursuing the ways of the Devil. And since the newly awakened often take on elf names, then many, if not most, of one's friends, will feel uncomfortable using this new name. At the same time the Elfae naturally wishes the name to be used to reinforce hir own confidence in pursuing the Elven Way. Each must decide in hir own circumstances how much sHe is willing, and how much it is wise, to reveal and to whom.

Those who feel the Call and who have awakened are faced with another challenge, for they come to understand they are truly Special Beings; they are the Chosen, or actually those who have

Chosen to pursue the Elven Way, and are in fact advanced souls and spirits relative to the mass of humanity at this point. They are truly elite beings, who have opened thems'elves and are dedicating thems'elves to developing their inner Soulfulness, and Spirit to become truly Cosmic Beings and to, in time, enter the Supra-Dimensional Realms where Faerie thrives in its fullness. The challenge here is how to know one is such a being without it enhancing the negative aspects of ego and leading thus to an increasing separation between the Elfae and those around hir who sHe is ultimately meant to help and guide. Thus each elf is called to remember that every being is a soulful being and each person contains the potential for greatness within hir, and is destined/designed to become hir own true s'elf in hir own time and way.

Although, the act of awakening and living one's elven nature often leads to those around us rejecting us, the Elfae must ever be conscious of not rejecting them in turn. The more we advance in our elven nature, and on the Path of Elven, the more sacred will we consider the souls of those around us, even if they, as yet, are not aware that they even have such a soul. Being one of the Elite should not separate us from others in our hearts, but make us ever more aware of being One with them. This struggle, however, with our own ego is often a life long process and the challenge of loving and accepting those who reject us, while at the same time protecting ours'elves from them, is a magic that often takes years, even lifetimes, to master. Fortunately, we live in Eternity and we have forever.

Of those who awaken, there tend to be two general types. First, and by far the greatest number, there are those who have heard the Call, but in fact have no idea of what to do about it. They sense that they are elven or other, but where to go from there, they know not. These tend to seek others who are already active and living their lives as elves, although it should be said that nearly all elves seek their kindred. We tend to be, for the most part, a very group oriented people. These are also the individuals who are most likely to cling to the religious and philosophical teachings of their past, and who often view Elfin from that perspective, that is to say they endeavor to merge their former religious ideas with their new sense of being Elven. There is nothing wrong with doing so, although this approach will only take one so far on one's journey into Faerie. This group are also the ones most likely to need leaders, at least for a while. They hunger for guidance. They are open, but don't know what to do with their openness, or whence to go. These are also those most likely to fall back into the world, fade from Elfin, or start pursuing a different, more popular fad. These, like many, perhaps most elves, hunger for love, connection and community and don't really care if it is called Elven or whatever; they just want to be loved, get laid (a lot), and have friends. Yet, even those who fade often come back to us in time. If someone is truly Called by Elfin, sHe will eventually find hir way there.

The second group of individuals who awaken to the Call, tend to be more creatively active. They often give thems'elves elf names, write their own faery tales, gather others about them, or attempt to do so (it is often hard to draw elves to one, we are an independent lot), and begin creating their own elvish culture, magic, and the implements and accessories there of. They are often leaders, but in the sense of being pioneers rather than authorities, and thus they are also more comfortable being solitary elves, although, as we've said previously, few elves like being solitary. These are also the Elfae most likely to continue on this Path long after everyone else around them have faded from it, and these individuals are usually less attached to traditional philosophies and religious notions. They have found the old ways wanting, and seek the Way of the Ancient Future. (Note elves often speak of the ancient future evoking Ancient Ways that are as yet unfilled, and are the Vision of evolutionary development.) However, these need to be careful that they don't merely substitute one dogma for another. The Paths to Elfin are many, and each has a right to find hir own way. Also, while the first type needs guidance and often fades if they don't find a confident elven soul to help them, this second sort need appreciation for their works and creations and may wander off if they don't get the recognition for which they hunger.

While we have written these as two distinct types for ease of understanding, and of which the second type tends to be more evolved in their elfin nature than the first. In reality, these types are often mixed individuals having a bit of both aspects in them, having some need for guidance and yet expressing some creative outpouring in need of recognition. And while the second type tends, as we say, to be more advanced or developed in their elven nature, that does not necessarily mean they are perfected souls and have no challenges of fate or karma, nor a need for personal transformation. Even very Adept kindred have aspects of personality they are striving to develop. Although, again these more evolved ones tend to have a more independent approach to Elfin, and often seem like they are making it all up as they go along, which, for the most part, they are. Although, we could also say they are channeling Faerie, or remembering it, that is to say drawing down memories of Elfin from our Collective Elven Unconscious.

Yet in saying this, we do not mean that anything goes. We do not mean one can disregard the precepts that make the Path to Elfin possible. Not all elves need involve thems'elves in magic, for instance, yet there is something essentially magical about Faerie, Elfin and the Elfae, and if one seeks to create an Elven world without magic, they have gone far astray. So it is, also, with prejudice. There simply cannot be an elven world that prohibits gays, males, females, blacks or anyone for their religious background, their race, gender, ethnicity, sexual preference, or any other aspect of being that they don't actually have any control over. We don't even have prejudice against the violent, the fanatical or the greedy, all of whom have a place in Faerie, although it is a dark and unfriendly place where various Unseelie reside, and most of us Seelie Elves avoid. And while they may find a place in Faerie, they will never evolve to the deeper reaches of Elfin until they do, indeed, master their own s'elves. No one can prevent anyone from entering the deeper regions of Faerie/Elfin, except the individual hir own s'elf by hir own behavior. No one has a right to say who is or isn't an elf, except the individual speaking for hir own s'elf, and yet certain behaviors will certainly keep one from finding those who could help one farther on the Path. We each must look into our own souls, examine our own personalities, and do what we feel best to develop ours'elves as spiritual beings.

This ultimately is a quest for the realization of our true S'elf, and we are called to rid ours'elves of every aspect of being, every behavior, every false notion about ours'elves and others that obstructs that realization. Therefore, while the Path of the Elfin seems to be but a fantasy to most folks, it is based upon a quest for truth about ours'elves, our true natures, and the true nature of the Universe. One needs only restrict ones'elf in so far as it is productive to the development of one's elven nature. All other restrictions are unnecessary and useless. We try to not judge others by the standards we have set for ours'elves, but by their consistency in living by the standards they have declared to be their own.

It is a paradox of the Elven Path that we must each find our own way, yet in the long run we can only do that together. Thus we seek to help each at the level sHe is at the moment. We do not expect, or demand, more than each is capable of giving or doing, but aid each as best we may, and as best we understand hir path. Curiously, by doing this we are both serving the individual and serving ours'elves. At the same time, one of the greatest things we can do for our Elfae kin is be our own true s'elves, thus we serve as an example to them, and therefore encourage them by this example, as well as actively seeking to empower them to do the same.

As yet, that is at the time of this writing, there are no great charismatic leaders in Elven Culture. Part of that is due to the fact that elves, by our nature tend to challenge authority and have an underlying streak of rebelliousness in our souls. "Question Authority" is not a motto for us, but a lifestyle. Although, it may more accurately be stated, "Question everything." And we do, sometimes to our own determent. Part of this lack of charismatic leadership is due to the fact that we are simply too much of a fringe society to have anyone charismatic bother trying to organize us, and as we say, we are somewhat loath to be organized. Like our Goth-Emo Pixie cousins, we are unlikely to ever become a part of mainstream society. Yet, in the ages to come, it is likely that such figures will emerge and an elf will only be safe in following such a being's lead in so much as these "leaders" encourage independent thought and action based upon the individual elf's sense of what is right for hirs'elf and hir others. Those who create stringent dogmas are not of us, have never been, and will never be so, until they evolve and become the inspiration for independent realization they are destined to be.

Coming to the Path

Just as there are two types that tend to hear the Call of Elfin so, too, are there two basic forces that lead one to Elfin; although, in this case these two often function in concert, both forces playing a pivotal role in one's readiness for the Awakening. The first of these forces is Attractive and the second Repulsive, and we do mean repulsive.

Elfin, Faerie, Elfland or the Sacred Realm or Dimension of Magic that lives at the heart of the Universe, is an incredibly attractive power. It draws all true souls to it. It calls to the Elfin nature in each and every soul. This is the power that arouses the imagination of those who see or read the *Lord of the Rings* and say, I'm an Elf or I'm a Dwarf, or even I'm an Orc. The power calls to us through Urban Fantasy stories and the fantasy novels of old, as well as, faery tales and movies of magic and enchantment. But it also calls to us from the trees, the wild places of Nature, and sometimes most of all from magic memories of our childhood, which is really our ancient past, our past incarnations, calling to us. It can also be aroused, and quite strongly, perhaps most strongly, by others of our kind manifesting in the world. There is something magical about these beings and they arouse our own hunger for magic in our own lives and souls. These Elfae radiate starlight. They glimmer with love, kindness and compassion; and they reach out and touch our souls. Some might suppose this to be a glamor, a magic they have wrapped thems'elves within to enchant us; but while they are truly enchanting, the magic arises from the fact that they are genuine and real. They don't need to glamor us. They just need to be their very own s'elves, for that is the most impressive magic of all. They are not trying, they are simply being: being thems'elves, being elves.

The second force is the Repulsive or Rejecting force. Most elves grow up in this world feeling alienated from those around us. When our peers (don't they wish) tell us we're weird, we take that to heart. When they say we are crazy, we say: yes we are, as we whisper to ours'elves, "…and you better watch out, mother fuckers". When they tell us we're odd, we believe them. And when they say we are different from them, we accept that as fact, and are glad of it. Elves seem to feel this more than most faerie folk. The faeries often find a way of appearing flighty, or "airy-fairy", and find acceptance in the world that way. But we elves, perhaps because we are slightly more serious in nature, or take ours'elves more seriously, accept that rejection of the world and embrace it. And while some of us strive at first to be accepted, most of us in time, discover it just isn't worth our effort. We're glad we are different from most folks, because honestly, they seem like a bunch of assholes to us. Are we being too blunt here? Should we decorate our language to appear cultured and highbrow? Make our words more flowery? Ah, but we are but simply elves really, with pixie blood, and bit a brownie in us, and perhaps a touch of this and that as well. We choose to be what we are without pretense rather than to pretend to appear to be what we are not. If some call us princes and princesses, kings and queens, that is very kind of them to be sure, and we are duly complimented by their kind thoughts and considerations; but we make no claims to be other than what we are, and what we are free to reveal. There are some magics best brewed in silence.

While the Attractive force is quite powerful, and clearly the more positive of the two forces, it is none-the-less limited in its nature. Having been attracted to Elfin, to elven culture and philosophy, then what? Can one spend all one's life wearing faerie wings to gatherings and never hunger for more? Perhaps some can, but not elves. Like nearly every soul, we seek the Truth. We seek the answers to the great questions such is: What is the Meaning of Life? Why do bad things happen to good people? Who are we really? And how did we get to be where we are? Is there a God, or some other intelligence power behind all this? The answers to most of these questions are only hinted at in Faery Tales and movies, and since our Elven People were long ago conquered and scattered, and our culture destroyed, where do we look for the answers to these questions? This book and our other books are an attempt to answer some of these questions; but usually, before we truly accept ours'elves as elves and look to elfin lore for answers, we look elsewhere. We try to understand our elfin nature and the spiritual nature of our being by searching the ancient texts of the various religious philosophies we've encountered. We tend to try the tried and purportedly true before we attempt a trek into the vast Unknown, into that Perilous Realm called Faerie.

There is certainly no harm in this, in fact, it is quite wise. However, sorting out what is true for us as elves and as individuals from what is mere fluff added on through the ages by others, ever calls for an inward search into our own feelings and instincts. Ultimately, what is true for us will always be decided by our own souls. At least, that is true for elves. Others may use their minds to decide, but we elves use our hearts. Which is not to say that we don't use our minds for critical examination of information presented to us, but in the end, we accept what feels right to us. That's how we know if something is Elven or close to it. Something may sound logical, but if it doesn't ring true in our hearts we cannot accept it. This is a lesson hard learned. There have been times when we ignored our feelings and only followed our head, but we've always suffered when we did so. Now, when our feelings/intuitions are aroused, we pay close attention to them.

The Repulsive force has a different effect on us than the attractive force. Particularly for those who feel alienated from Normal society and yet have not, as yet, found any elven kin with whom to relate, this can be an awful time. One feels outcast and alone in the world with no one to turn to, and no one who understands. This often leads to what is generally called the Dark Night of the Soul, and many an elf has contemplated suicide in this depressing phase of hir existence. One casts about for connection and, it is at this time also when one is liable to become involved with this or that cult, seeking others who share one's sense of rejection. Until we find our elven kin, we elves often flit from spiritual group to spiritual group, or from fad to fad (usually hoping to get laid, but also seeking the truth).

It is true that as time goes on, and more and more Elfae manifest in the world, this will become less of a problem. Elves will find other elves near about. But the quest for the inner secrets, the Truth of the World, and the true Magic will go ever on. And even in a world that is filled with Faerie Folk there will still be advanced brothers and sisters who will hunger to know more, too see "behind the veil" and know the truth of their nature and the True Nature of the Universe. This is a never-ending Quest; behind every veil there is another one.

There are those who will ever be satisfied with the opinions of others on these subjects, on what they have been taught since childhood, or what their peers say, but these are not elves. Each elf examines the world from hir own perspective. It is not that each elf rejects what sHe has been taught, but neither does sHe automatically accept it. It must, first and foremost, make sense in hir own heart, in hir feelings and understanding of the world. Elves always examine the world as a whole, and seek to integrate all we know into our worldview, because we have an inner sense of the unity of Life and Nature.

At the same time, we elves are not inclined to argue with anyone about our understanding of the Universe, or our philosophical views. We know that each one must come to the Truth in hir own way and time, and we know, even better, that we have changed our own views many times, and are likely to do so again when more and better information reveals itself, greater reasoning prevails, more profound revelations illuminate us and higher Initiation occurs. We are not set in our views, except for the fact that we are determined in the idea that our views are ever evolving and open to greater understanding. Yet it is clear to us that one must be consistent in one's views, which is to say one needs to integrate all one's knowledge into a consistent whole, and that one needs to live one's beliefs. One's acts must be consistent with one's opinions. Each elf feels the need to live hir magic, to make it real though hir life. While one may begin by pretending to be an elf, and this is a result of the Attractive force drawing one to Elfin even before one actually believes in it, every elf comes to a place where in hir heart and soul, she needs to make it real through hir life and actions. We want Elfin to be real, not just fantasy, and we make it real by living it. This is magic, the magic of Being. We are not pretending to be elves, although that can be fun, too. We are Being elves, manifesting as elves, and thus bringing our elven lives into being. All true magic stems from our Being, is actualized by our actions, empowered by our will, and shaped by our intent.

It is clear to we elven as well that whatever answers we come up with concerning life, whatever religious or spiritual beliefs we have, must be consistent with the facts of Nature, which we come to understand primarily through Science. There is a caveat with this however in that the Laws of Nature as it exists out among the Stars can differ from the Laws of Nature on this Planet, and Science while a valuable guide is, like we elven, ever changing its views based on new information. Also, Science, or really modern Scientists tend to look at the world primarily from a materialistic standpoint, and our elven understanding of the Universe incorporates experiences and dimensions that, as yet for the most part, are elusive to current scientific examination and research (although Quantum Physics approaches it). Thus as elves, while we don't deny or contradict science, we are ever seeking to go beyond what Science knows into the vast unknown that lives beyond its understanding.

Science deals mostly with the mechanical aspects of the Universe, cause and effect, how things work and why. We elves, however, are also called to examine such things as morality and the psyche and soul of the individual, the spirit of the individual, and what is real and true beyond the temporary manifestation of a particular life. What is our true s'elf? What is it that survives us as we transition from one body to another shedding our previous body and all the memories that are linked to it in our brains? Which leads us back ever to who are we truly?

Is the Universe merely a random comingling of elements? Is there purpose to life? Or does it even matter what we do in life, except to succeed in this life? Is there really such a thing as Karma? Or can we do anything we want as long as we get away with it? As many folks seem to believe, or certainly act. Is there any value in acting morally, or having a conscience (a word these elves haven't heard used very much in a very long time)?

And if we are truly Immortal Beings, as the Faery Tales and legends tell us we are, of what does that Being consist? What of us is Immortal? Not the temporary manifestation of our current bodies, surely, not our ideas, our opinions, or our memories (as senility, dementia and Alzheimer's assure us). And if not these things, then what? Our Soul? But if our Soul is immortal, what is our Soul? For now, we will merely say that we will define soul in a circular fashion. What is immortal in our nature? Our soul. And what is our soul? It is our immortal nature. Of what does this Soul consist? Spirit. And what is spirit? It is the energetic aspect that composes our soul. And how do we know this? S'elf Knowledge, and what is s'elf knowledge, it is the conscious awareness of our soulful spirit, our Beingness, the part of us that is, ever and always, and to which we, by choice and through our actions, shape, clothe with energy and through our experiences, make unique.

If we are not to be mere automatons, or robots in this world, and this idea is one that serves to repel elves from the world, (which is in part why elves hate the idea of being work-slaves and thus often despise the current notion of work) we elves must not only think for ours'elves, but feel for ours'elves, we must be true to what is true within us and value that above all other things. As we have written elsewhere, and it is in fact engraved in runes on the sacred cliffs of Elfin, it is not the name Elf that makes us elves, it is the uniqueness of our natures that does so, and it is this uniqueness that we share, and that unites us, with all our others. To become aware of one's unique and individual nature, to think for ones'elf, and be true to one's pure feelings, is to step upon the Path that leads inevitably to Elfin.

The Will to Mastery

Just as there are two general types of individuals who hear the call to Elfin, and two ways that this Call evokes to draw or impel us toward it, so also the soulful elfin spirit encounters two forms of Will, the first of these we might call the Automatic, Robotic or Animal Will, and the second of these is the Will to Mastery. It is this second Will that each individual, whether elf or other, invokes when they hear the Call to spiritual development and seek to rise above being a mere reactive agent in the world, propelled endlessly by hir passions and desires. In mastering ours'elves, that is to say our bodies, minds, emotions, impulses, etc. we begin to master the world.

Before we proceed on this topic, let us say that unlike many religious doctrines that deny that animals have souls, we elves see soulfulness pervading the all of Life. We are essentially Animists. Everything is alive and all things have soul, however, some things, like a chair or an automobile, while composed of life are not, at this point at least, organically soulful, that is to say they do not as yet have an individual soul but instead consist of smaller souls, atoms that have been molded together. However, it is not beyond possibility, in the elfin mind, that in some other dimension they have souls, or that they will in time develop souls as things evolve in this dimension.

Usually, these inorganic objects, which do not have a governing soul of their own, are potential vessels for Spirit or spirits. Just as we can live in our houses, so can a spirit use a statue or some other object to live within. In the elven mind, when something like a sword is given a name, as Excalibur in the King Arthur legends was, it begins in earnest its journey toward becoming an integrated and soulful spirit. It comes alive so to speak, or takes on a life of its own.

These elves, for instance, have a teapot we call Miss Teal. It is just a petty little teal colored teapot that we use occasionally for brewing a special Japanese tea our son and daughter-in-law give us. But by giving Miss Teal a name and anthropomorphizing her we have created a thought form that will one day, probably not even in this cycle of evolutionary development, lead her through the stages of organic life until Miss Teal finds hers'elf (she is after all an elfin teapot) in some dimension serving tea regularly to others (probably to elves). From whence she will evolve from there will be mainly up to her, but having been created she will continue (theoretically) to evolve.

So, also, in viewing the trees and animals, we elves appreciate their soulful life. We do not, as mankind and many others seem to do, kill them with impunity, regardless of their life force. They are not here for us to do with as we will, as many religious types seem to think; they are not our possessions that we might destroy at whim. They are also souls on the path of evolution, and while they may not be as advanced as we, they still deserve our respect and, in as much as possible, our assistance in their evolutionary journey. This is in part why most evolved elves tend to be vegetarian.

Animal life, while intelligent, none-the-less, is limited by its current evolutionary status, and for the most part is reflective of the first type of Will, or really, the undeveloped Will that tends to manifest in our earliest incarnations and is necessary to keep us going and move us toward the great goals of life that we, at that point, are unable to comprehend intellectually.

If we follow the adage As Above/So Below, or as we elves often say As Within/So Without, life on the micro scale is reflective of the macro scale and the nature of Faerie is reflected in the worlds and dimensions surrounding it. So just as the body has an Automatic Nervous System that controls most bodily functions including in its Sympathetic function, the urge toward fight or flight, our "lower" or undeveloped Will is automatic. It reacts to life events, and pursues our drives, desires, and passions. But we also have aspects of our body that we control by Will, such as walking, looking about, and reaching out, and so forth, and this is reflective of a higher, more evolved Will, the Will that wishes to reach beyond mere reaction, or passion and desire driven life toward the life of Mastery and Spiritual development. We seek to gain power over ours'elves and our lives and not be mere powerless puppets awash in a Universe of events beyond our control. This is the true purpose of our magic.

We might say the difference between them is the difference between riding on a bus and driving a car. In riding the bus, the lower Will — something other than ours'elves — directs our progress, while in driving a car we are in control of our journey. This is particularly true of the lowest aspects of our being, and those least evolved in, or as yet not having, higher Will; however, for most of us who are more evolved but not totally free of the influence of overruling passions and desires, the difference is like the distinction between driving a cable car and driving an automobile. In the cable car, we have very limited control of our vehicle, whereas in a car, we have much greater control. Most people in the world today are on the level of driving a cable car, only very few, and very developed souls, come near to the level of driving that car.

Yet, as we obtain that power and proficiency in directing our higher Will, or the higher aspects of our Will, we also obtain greater freedom and power, as is obvious by the above examples. This does not mean we are free to simply drive however we wish, although we are indeed free to do so, as the Dark Lodge knows, but it is as unwise to do so as it is to go around deliberately smashing into other cars, or trees or buildings. This higher power of Will, with its increased freedom of movement and choice, also carries with it greater responsibility, particularly a responsibility to act in a cooperative fashion with the rest of evolving life. This, as we will see, is also in our own best interests.

Some seem to think that the opposite is true, that the lower will compels us to wild and uncontrolled animal urges and that in rising to the Mastery of Will we surrender our Will to God. In their minds the only freedom we have is to obey or disobey God's commandments, whatever they deem them to be according to their particular religion or sect. And, as ever, there is some truth to this, in that the animalistic desires and passions of our lower s'elf, or Will, do often lead us to do things that involve conflict and create chaos. But the Universe is more creative than that, and ever in a continual process of balancing itself. Just as in the example of driving a cable car or an automobile, as we move toward Mastery of the Will we do gain more freedom, but we also begin to see ever more clearly how our freedom depends upon cooperation and mutual respect. Also, and this is vital, we increasingly come to understand that what we desire, what truly fulfills us, is also what the Universe and the Higher Spirits, that is to say the more evolved spirits, that these elves call the Shining Ones, wish for us. It is simply in our own best interests to cooperate with the Plan of Evolutionary development.

The Plan

What then is the Plan? The Plan involves the evolution and empowerment of every individual, which is to say bringing the all of life into conscious realization and cooperative, which means loving, union. Ultimately, you become who you truly are, which is also who you truly wish to be. You become your true s'elf while helping others do the same. And yet, the way most folks currently define thems'elves is but a very pale reflection of what their true s'elves are. They misinterpret the temporary and the transitory for the Eternal.

We are ever becoming more. How is this possible to become more and still be ours'elves? Because we, like Faerie its'elf, make all things our own. This is the Elven Way. This is the Plan.

A Few Words About the Dark Lodge

The Dark Lodge, also sometimes called the Black Lodge, which among the elfin are called usually the Unseelie Folk, is composed of individuals who have progressed in the Mastery of the higher Will but who, as yet, refuse to cooperate with the Plan. They are often pictured as being evil, and in fact they often create very painful circumstances for people in the world, and thus ultimately for their own s'elves because everything we do comes back to us eventually (the laws of karma and magic). The Dark Lodge functions rather like the Mafia. That is to say they have a strict hierarchy that is enforced through violence or the threat of violence, and all wealth tends to flow upwards. They cooperate with each other because they need to do so, yet they will kill those around them, or above them, or below them, if they think they can profit from it and get away with it. (Note: there is no getting away with it in the Eternal, but it seems that way sometimes in the transitory nature of a particular lifetime. Everything we do comes back to us. This is the Law of Magic. It is the nature of Reality and there is no way, except temporarily of getting around it. Those who mistake the temporary for the Eternal often make this error.)

Again, the Unseelie are often portrayed as evil, but in fact they are merely individuals who have developed a certain mastery over their lower will but as yet have not evolved to the point where they realize the true benefits of cooperation. They are still greatly affected by the hierarchal aspects of the animal regions, which is to say the Food-Chain, and they are driven to be the Apex Predators in order to survive and succeed. This is at great cost to their psyches and their souls, and if continued for too many lifetimes will returned them to animal existence, or even in time to inorganic existence, but that seldom happens. Usually, they just continue to suffer and cause suffering until they learn a better way.

However, the Dark Lodge is essentially anti-evolutionary by nature. They wish to dominate others rather than uplift them. They seek to rise at the expense of others, and thus are in conflict with the Great Plan that seeks to uplift everyone and every aspect of life.

The Goals of Evolutionary Life

There are two primary goals of life. The first of these is Immortality. The second is Happiness. There is a third and overriding goal but we will get to that in a moment. We are driven to live forever. In the lowest form, that is the lower aspect of Will, we see this as the Will to survive at nearly any cost. Thus nearly every being acts to preserve and extend its life as much as possible. This does not require the higher Will, it is implanted as an automatic function of our lower Will. Therefore, deliberate suicide while unfortunate, usually occurs as the individual gains a certain amount of Mastery over the Will, and influences other than mere survival, such as social standing, begin to take precedence.

The second main goal of Life is Happiness, which can also be seen, particularly in the lower aspects as Success. We are all driven to succeed in life, which at certain times means to Survive, and we all desire happiness, even if some individuals have temporarily come to be wired to confuse pain and misery with happiness. And we also wish this Happiness to last forever, which connects it with the drive toward Immortality.

We do not wish to live forever in pain or to be forever miserable, a state that many religions and sects threaten us with if we don't follow their chosen mode of worship and living. And this idea, that one will be miserable forever, or the rest of hir life, is the cause of most suicides. It is also, of course, the threat of Hell Eternal that is so often used to browbeat weak willed or weak-minded individuals into social conformity.

So we don't wish to live forever in misery, and we also want our happiness to last forever, thus we wish for a Life of Eternal Happiness. This is reflected in the typical Fairy Tale ending: "And They Lived Happily Ever After." This is the true goal of evolution, and it is hard wired into every living being. It is also the Promise that Faerie holds out to us.

There is a third aspect, a third drive, although it is a hidden aspect, which forms the Holy Trinity or family of drives. It is so obvious it goes mostly unseen. This is the urge toward Conscious Realization. It is unseen because it is so apparent that it hardly needs noticing. We wish to live happily ever after, and we wish to be conscious doing so. We don't wish, like Sleeping Beauty to be in a blissful but unknowing slumber forever. We want to experience our happiness; we wish to know that we are happy; we hunger to be conscious and aware. And as we say, this is so clearly true it hardly needs to be mentioned.

The typical gravestone R. I. P. "rest in peace" is an indication of our lack of knowledge, understanding and faith concerning the true nature of Life and the Universe. Although, it is also an indication of an unconscious knowledge that Death is but another form of Sleep.

The Evolving Aspect of Will

In most beings, these drives toward Immortality, Happiness and Sentient Consciousness are inherent. We wish to survive, we wish to succeed at whatever we desire, to get what we want, and when we are very young, at least, we wish to stay awake for it all. But as we evolve we begin to realize that merely pursuing our immediate desires and passions do not always lead us to the greater success for which we hunger.

Therefore in the lower aspects of Will the drive toward pleasure and success, which is to say the fulfillment of our desires, usually also involves the avoidance of pain. Thus in the simplest form pleasure is good, and pain bad. We are attracted to those things that give us pleasure, and we avoid or are repelled by things that cause pain.

However, in time we realize that life is more complicated than that, and we find that things that give us pleasure in the short run, such as smoking cigarettes or doing drugs, or overeating, etc. can cause us terrible pain later on. And things which give us pain temporarily, such as getting a shot at the doctor's, going to the dentist, or even working out (no pain, no gain), can save us greater suffering later.

Thus we come in time to realize that by developing the will and limiting our desires and passions, we gain in pleasure and usually increase our chances of living longer. We substitute temporary pleasure for long-term pleasure. It is in our souls' and our bodies' best interests to develop the Will, which is to say to Master our desires, drives and passions. Thus the urge to develop Magical powers, which nearly every elf experiences, is simply the desire to Master our Will, have greater success in Life, which means happiness and also to Live Forever, or as long as possible. Magic is after all, our power to use our Will to achieve what we wish in life. In Elf Speak that means, making our wishes come true. This is, in fact, one of the most common themes in fairy tales, the ability of Elfae to grant wishes, or make dreams come true.

This brings us back to the contrast between the robotic slavery of being driven by uncontrolled passions in life and the s'elf limiting freedom of Mastering one's Will. The I Ching (Wilhelm/Baynes translation) advises us that we become free spirits in life by deciding for our own s'elves what our duty is. We are free to cooperate with the Plan or not, however, as we've stated earlier, it is in our best interests to so cooperate, for the plan is the creative realization of our own soulful spirits. The more we willingly cooperate, the more successful we become and the greater freedom we have within that cooperative system.

The Seeming Conflict

As we've said, there are not really two Wills but one that evolves. However, it may seem as if there are two wills as the passionate drives which originate from the lower aspect of the will resists the efforts of this higher aspect of Will to assert itself. This becomes even more complicated by the influx of the mind that attaches ideas and opinions to feelings, which thus create emotions. These emotions are not pure feeling and they tend to be reactionary by nature.

Therefore as many seek the development of their Will, they often do so through spiritual and religious groups that instill them with ideas about the way things should be, which then get attached to religious feelings and become emotions, sometimes of a positive sort, sometimes of a destructive type. There are also social and ethnic beliefs that have the same effect.

This often creates a conflict between the basic drives, such as the drive toward happiness and immortality that manifest in the sexual urge as a drive toward pleasure and procreation, with beliefs such as one should only have sex when married, or only with those to whom one is married, or only with those of the same race, gender, religion, culture, etc. This attempt to limit the desires often comes into conflict with the desires themselves, and this creates in most individuals a Shadow self that emerges when one is inebriated or loses control of the Will under stress. A conflict thus arises between the lower bodily driven aspects of will and the aspiration toward the higher will, which is driven by what it perceives or has been told are higher ideals.

This leads us to societies where individuals go to church and espouse peace while at home they beat their wives, promote war with other nations, are prejudiced against minorities, or do underhanded business deals to get ahead while essentially ripping off or exploiting others, all under the guise of being good Christians, Moslems, or whatever. Because this creates a conflict within them, and because nearly all beings are essentially wired to promote what is good and just or fair in society, these individuals then must rationalize those actions that conflict with the those principles that they have adopted as being higher spiritual or moral values. This is an attempt to ease the Cognitive Dissonance that their conflicting aspects of Will have created. Many folks resolve this dilemma by simply not looking at the conflict, by separating the contrasting aspects of their lives and failing, or refusing, to examine and integrate these conflicting elements. In other words, they deal with it by not dealing with it.

What adds to the confusion is the fact that some of these dogmas that have been created by religious groups are really the directives of the Dark Lodge seeking to control the individual for their (the Dark Magicians) benefit, rather than that of the individual, and are only posing as true aspects of developed Will. However, since these aspects, even while erroneous, do encourage the individual to develop Mastery, they tend to lead the individual to eventual realization. It is said that for the earliest Initiations for Adepts, the training for the Dark Lodge and that of the Vortex of Light, is identical, thus you will sometimes find eventual Dark Sorcerers training among the Champions of Light as well as finding those who tend toward the Dark who realize the Higher Aspects of Evolutionary development and join the Vortex of Light, the magical Lodge of the Shining Ones, our Ancient Elven Ancestors who have evolved into the Supra-Dimensions.

This is why, even though the Dark Lodge or the Unseelie, create suffering in the short run, and tend to imploded and destroy thems'elves and each other in the long run (being essentially parasitic), they are also valuable in promoting the development of the Will, even if it is done upon false or illusionary precepts. You will discover in time that the Shining Ones turn all things, all events and circumstances to their advantage. There is a place for everyone in the Great Plan.

The Dark Lodge, or the Unseelie, are Dominance oriented. They view the world like an organization where the individual at the top gives the orders and everyone else follows them. This, however, does not always make for a very efficient organization. It can be very quick in terms of making changes, however, it can be very slow in terms of effectively responding to anything that is new and not already in its range of programming, for everything needs to be sent to the top for a decision to be made. Try dealing with almost any bureaucracy, governmental or corporate.

The Vortex of Light is like an organization where every individual is an expert in hir chosen area and makes decisions for hirs'elf in any evolving situation. This, however, requires an incredible sense of cooperation in order to make large-scale changes. Therefore the idea of voluntarily getting with the Plan is highly emphasized here. In the Dark Lodge you simply have to obey orders or suffer for failing to do so. In many ways that is much easier, particularly for those who do not wish to carry the burden of responsibility. Bureaucracies are filled with individuals of this type and this makes them, for the most part, incredibly inefficient.

This top down aspect of leadership ends up demanding tremendous amounts of micromanaging. Having each person be an effective master on hir own level, which is the goal of the Great Plan, is much more effective way of doing things in the long run. Although, it requires that the leadership ability in every individual be developed. Whereas the Dark Lodge only needs, and will only tolerate, one strong leader with eager subordinates, and many, many followers.

Take the idea of micromanaging one's body. There are yogis who can control their breath, their heart rate and various other bodily functions, and this is surely something that can lead to great power and be necessary at times, just as it is good for the owner or CEO of a company to know the workings of all the departments under hir care. But, we wouldn't want to control our breath all the time. It is much more efficient to let the automatic nervous system that controls these things to continue to do so. We would only intervene if needed. So, also, the Universe and the Vortex of Light, or the Seelie Elves, and the Shining Ones wish us to control our own lives and destiny. They don't want to micromanage our lives, which would be horribly inefficient; they simply need us to cooperate with the Great Plan, which as we say is to our benefit anyway.

Knowing the Plan

But the question arises, how do we distinguish what truly is in accordance with the Great Plan, or as we elves call it the Path to Faerie, if there are so many spiritual and religious groups, cults and sects, as well as ethnic and social pressures and influences all telling us different things, and some of them designed to mislead us? And we add to that the fact that our own desires drive us into conflict with our higher Will, but also into conflict with these false doctrines. How do we know one from the other?

The first response and the one very commonly heard is we must trust our own s'elf. And this is true, although it is again complicated by the fact that we are often not clear about what constitutes that s'elf and what are in fact Introjects, that is spells inculcated into us usually at a very early age, and are aspects of enculturation, which are not truly us but may appear to be so since they speak within our own minds. Not to mention the fact that what seems to be our s'elf is often our desire and passion driven body.

In extreme cases, these Introjects take the form of Dark Spells that drive individuals to violence, which these plagued individuals often refer to as the Devil speaking inside them. They, while they do not exercise proper resistance against these demons, none the less recognize them for what they truly are, and don't mistake these spells for themselves speaking, although psychiatrists may seek to convince them otherwise.

Yet, despite these facts, the answer remains, first and foremost, that we must come to trust our own S'elves in the form of our instincts and intuitions, which so many refer to as listening to our hearts. However, many confuse their heart with their passions and desires, and we need to clarify what actually comes from our hearts, intuition and instincts. And to do that we need to discover what that S'Elf truly is.

The Underlying Assumption

We posit a basic assumption that almost all souls are essentially good, that is to say they support and hunger for fairness and justice. Even criminals who have committed dozens of crimes often feel that they have been treated unfairly if the police tamper with the evidence to convict them, or they are convicted of a crime they didn't actually commit. Curiously, criminals tend in many ways to be more socially conservative than most people. It is true there are some individuals who have been so damaged by their upbringing that they are like a car with no brakes or with bad steering. They simply can't be trusted and unless repaired, and alas most societies are better at damaging children than repairing that damage, are dangerous to be around or let loose. But this is not because they are basically evil people, but because karma and fate have created a life of suffering for them, and others with whom they have come into contact. We are not saying that their deeds are not their own fault, but at the same time there is no question that we are often shaped by our environment and upbringing. For the Elf, the magician, and the adept, initiation begins when one ceases to blame others for what one does, although they may indeed bear great blame and karma, and one assumes responsibility for one's own life. The Path of Initiation, the Path of the Elven, is accepting the fact that we are shaped by circumstances while gaining control over our own responses, rather than merely reacting, and thus achieving power and true magic in our lives. We can't always control the circumstances in our lives, although the Stars know most of us try, but we can gain increasing power over our own s'elves and through that s'elf control affect the world, as we will see as we continue.

So, let's go back to our basic assumption that all people are essentially good if they have developed at all any aspect of higher Will. If they function only on lower Will then they are merely reactive animals pursuing passion and desire as well as seeking to fulfill the great Drives of Life, that is Immortality and Happiness, in its lowest forms, which manifest on that level as survival and simple pleasure. Thus, they are truly pawns to these demons of desire. When we say good, we mean that they want what is best for thems'elves, that is they want to succeed, and know essentially, that is to say know in their core beings, that what is best for them is also best for others at the same time that what is best for others is also best for them. We know that many seek only their own 'good', seek to profit at the expense of others, but in the course of evolution and initiation we will come to understand that we cannot really succeed without our others. Or if we do we will be all alone in a deep black hole we have created for ourselves.

So how do we come to that place where we can access our basic "goodness", or really our purity of being, to know our true s'elves?

Meditation

The sages tell us that calming our minds, and thereby slowing down our thinking processes, will help us to reduce the endless chatter of thought, give us greater control over our emotions and lower drives, and bring us in touch with our pure feeling nature, rather than our emotions. This pure feeling nature becomes obscured and overwhelmed by ceaseless mind chatter linked to emotional and passionate arousal and fantasies. Understand, we are not saying there is anything essentially wrong about passionate arousal or fantasies, however, we need to be in control of them, in the sense of guiding and directing them, rather than being driven uncontrollably by them.

That meditation can be effect for this is certainly the case and we highly recommend elves using meditation to access their inner s'elves. Still, having achieved that, one must come to the essential trust of one's s'elf. One must use one's pure feelings, that is non-desire driven feelings, or one's intuition as a guide to what is right or wrong for one's own s'elf at any particular time or circumstance. Because, it is quite possible and frequently true, that what is right for one at one point in life may no longer be the right direction to pursue at another time in life. And that what is right for one individual may be very wrong for another. Thus we ever keep in mind the method of the scientist who explores from what sHe knows into the unknown holding in hir consciousness the reality that further facts and evidence may lead hir to different conclusions farther down the way. Remember the path to Elfin weaves through the forest of life.

In other words, each elf needs to decide for hir own s'elf what is right for hir at any particular moment and circumstance, ever keeping in mind the guidance of hir own conscience and what seems to be fair and right for hir and all others. Elves come to trust that we pursue the goals and interests that we do, because we are Who we are. And we come to distrust, or examine very critically, those who tell us we should be other than we know ours'elves to be.

Before we proceed, however, let us note that there are essentially two methods of meditation. The first we might call cleansing, or Zen meditation, which seeks to continually clear the mind of thoughts, observing one thought after another, but not following or lingering on any of them, simply noting and dismissing them one after the other, ever seeking the place of silence. The second we may call Shamanic meditation, which uses a mantra to focus and concentrate the mind and is essentially a form of spell casting that involves repetitive chanting. We might use the metaphor of a radio to describe these two. The first type of meditation removes static so we will have a clear channel, and eventually be able to receive the voice of the Universe without conflicting channels. The other, the shamanic meditation, is like broadcasting on a radio, sending out a repetitive signal, and magically seeking a receptive audience. Both serve to focus the mind. Note that repetitive drumming and or dancing are often used in coordination with this second meditation. Particularly note our spiritual kin the Sufis.

But how do we know what we conceive of as our true s'elf is in keeping with the Great Plan? There are certainly plenty of people in the world who are eager to tell us we shouldn't be doing what we are doing, and instead should do what they think we should do. These are not only prolific, but usually quite vocal. And how do we distinguish what is right and fair in the world?

The Wiccan Rede

The Wiccan Rede is: And it harm none, do what you will. We love it. We would rewrite it and make it elven but it's already perfect. Why fix what isn't broken? In fact, we love it so much we can't help but think it originated from the elves. But then we elves think nearly everything cool originated with us. The Wiccan Rede is certainly in keeping with the great goals of the Universe and the Universal Laws.

So this is the essential guide. You have a right, in fact a duty, to pursue your own interests as long as you don't harm others. Why a duty? Because you were created by the Universe to be yours'elf, thus in pursuing your own interests you are doing what you were created to do. Some might say that we weren't created, we just happened by accident. But the essential fact remains the same, you are an individual and this is how you are meant to be. You can chose to forgo your individuality, to be like everyone else, to become ever more robotic. That is surely your choice to make. However, in the long run we discover that everyone else is also an individual, and deciding to be like them leads us eventually to be our own s'elves.

This does not mean however that you are obligated to lead a selfish life. It may be that you have come to the point where you have realized your oneness with the all of life, or a greater potion of life around you, and understand that what you are interested in and what is in your s'elf interest is service and helping others. This is for you to decide. But know this. You are made to be and become your true s'elf, and it is your duty to ever perfect that s'elf hood. Your s'elf interests and the perfection of your s'elf are also in the best interests of everyone else.

Note, however, that there are always people who are willing, even eager, to tell you that what you may wish to do will harm them, or their delicate sensibilities. You can't run around naked in most societies because there are those who claim they, and their children, would be harmed by seeing nudity. We find their arguments lacking, and we know they are using this to force others to conform to their ideas of what society should be like, and among elves nudity is widely accepted, although in fact you will find most of us dressed in what normal society considers costumes, and we consider style. Still, every elf with a modicum of wisdom learns to conform, at least on the surface, to the social prejudices of the society they find thems'elves within. This is not only wise and courteous, but also, as we've come to learn through the millennia, the only safe way to proceed. It is simply a fact that we often find ours'elves living in the midst of individuals who are prone to prejudice, ignorance and sometimes resort to savage violence to enforce their particular cultural morés. As the old elf saying goes: when in Rome, do as the Romans do, or they may punch you out.

This argument that someone else's freedom will harm my own, however, is the same argument that is, at this writing, being used to oppose same sex marriage, claiming that it will harm heterosexual marriage if allowed. These same arguments were used to oppose marriage between different races, and at one time, different religions and ethnic groups. There are always those who wish to limit others by claiming that what those others do will harm them. These arguments are spurious and in time they come to be seen as being so by the majority of individuals who, again, have a basic inclination to doing what is right and fair, which they come to realize is in their own long-term interests. But in the meantime, most of us adapt publicly while carrying on opposition to such injustices. The real question comes down to: is the other really actually harmed by your actions?

Astrology

Another way elves use to understand their own natures and come to understand the Great Plan as it concerns their own s'elves, is Astrology. Every elf advancing toward Mastery and Adeptship, as well as every Occultist and Esotericist, is well advised to learn at least the basic rudiments of Astrology and how to cast a simple natal and progressed chart. There is much that can be gleaned from Astrology.

However, as old as Astrology is, and it is a very old science, is still far from developed to it fullest extent and the successful interpretation of a chart often depends upon the ability of the individual practitioner. And even though medical science and even automobile mechanics are, at this time, more commonly accepted and developed fields, that same can be said of them as well. Often it depends on how good your doctor, or your auto mechanic, is. This is certainly true of Psychology and Psychiatry that, like Astrology, have a long way to go before being at the level of development where they will be practiced widely with great proficiency. Still, learning astrology or knowing one's charts, both natal and progressed, can be very helpful in understanding one's current lessons, challenges and place in the Universe. And this is one of Astrology's great benefits; it helps us see beyond one particular lifetime and to begin to comprehend the evolutionary nature of reality.

However, this is still information coming to you from without, and you are ever brought back to the fact that you must decide for yours'elf what really rings true for you.

Elven Kin

So it is also the case that many of us, perhaps most of us are influenced and guided by those who make an impression upon us. We often model ours'elves, particularly when we are young, on movie stars, rock stars, saints or other great spiritual or magical beings, both actual and those born of fantasy. But the greatest influences often come from those we know personally who awaken something within us.

Again, we must use our own intuition, and natural attraction, to decide which individuals meet this criterion, although in truth there are certain individuals who just evoke something within us. And this is usually how the awakening to our elven nature occurs. We meet an elf, or elves, manifesting in hir elven nature and we're like ... wow! We can't help ours'elves. They touch us to our core.

It is true that sometimes Elfin calls to the Elfae through movies, books, or other means, but the true transmission of the Elfin Magic and the Awakening nearly always takes place in person from one elf to another. These are individuals of Power who affect us by their mere presence without any effort to do so. And when we begin to intuitively and instinctually trust these individuals (although they may not be totally perfected thems'elves) we also find them to be a valuable guide to understanding our true s'elves, and the Path to Elfin and the Elven Way.

This, however, as each of us finds, does not relieve us of the responsibility of deciding for our own s'elves what our true course is. They are, great as they may be, only examples and guides. As much as we may admire others, this path is about the development of our own true s'elves. However, in doing so we find that we progress on the Path most easily and quickly when we assist others in doing the same and are so assisted.

Integration of our Natures

As we develop ours'elves we become more and more integrated as individuals. As we said previously, there are those who lack integration in their lives, they say they are Christian but fail to live the precepts of Christianity. The more elfin we become in our nature the more important it is that we are integrated in our personalities, what is commonly referred to as "walking our talk". This is also our means of judging the integrity of others, that is we ever look at how well they live up to the ideals they espouse, but first and foremost we look to our own s'elves, and our own integration. In understanding our own lack of perfection, we also come to develop a certain amount of compassion for others who are less than perfected.

This integration of the s'elf involves not only bringing our ideals into coordinated balance with our actions, but it also serves to help integrate the shadow aspects of our s'elves, of our unconscious, with our conscious s'elf. This is a process Carl Jung called Individuation, and for good reason, for the more integrated we become as individuals, the more in tune with our true nature, the more we rid ours'elves of the spells of enculturation and the overriding passions and desires that arise therefrom; and the more effectively then do we gain direction over our lives and become truly unique beings as we are meant and destined to be.

Let us take a moment to examine the aspects that compose our natures.

The Body

Most people look at the world from a materialistic viewpoint. Everything revolves around their physical being. Our emotions and thoughts are biochemical reactions and everything depends upon the physical body. In this worldview, all things originate from the physical plane. From a spiritual viewpoint, the opposite is actually true. All things originate from the planes of spirit, or subtle planes of energy, and the material world is a reflection of that energy. But ultimately there is no real conflict here, for these plans of being, which are separated by our minds in order to analyze and understand them, are really all of one essence.

As we know, or as modern scientists tell us, our bodies are composed of atoms. In one sense, the human body is mostly water, in another sense, it is mostly space since the atoms that compose us are mostly space. But in actuality, we are energetic beings, and our bodies are, at present, a temporary composition of that energy. We are Life. We are Consciousness. We are Awareness. Our body is a reflection of that consciousness.

Feelings

The feelings arise out of the body's sense organs. The sense of touch, taste, sight, smell and hearing are the most physical feelings/sensations. As the feelings interact with the mind, or thoughts, they create emotions, and as they are purified and become in touch with greater reality, they develop into intuition and from there, psychic perception. The feelings are our link to all that is within and beyond us, thus in this way our feelings, our ability to feel, sympathize, have compassion, have passion, has often been associated with our Soulful nature. We will speak more of the Soul, later.

Our feelings let us know what is going on in and to our bodies and connects us with those in our immediate environment as well as those we have known in the past. They function as an extension of our consciousness.

Thoughts

Thoughts or ideas arise out of the differentiation of experience. As thought develops it expands into systems of ideas and ideals. Higher thought becomes pure conscious awareness. When we integrate our being we are not merely integrating our thoughts with our actions, but our thoughts and feelings. When these elements are not integrated it creates cognitive dissonance, which causes stress within the being. The being, the body seeks homeostasis and harmony within itself, however most people achieve that state by rationalizing and the being is thus further split instead of truly integrated since the harmonization of the ideas are then based on false premises that cover up the underlying reality. Since stress is a key factor in disease or the lowering of the immune system, it should be clear that the true integration of the s'elf also inclines one towards better health. Thus while some might think that elves have the gift of longevity due to their bodies being different than man's, we'd say that the tendency toward long life of the elves is due, in great part, to the integration of our psyches.

Soul

So what is this thing we call soul? And why does the devil want to buy it from us? The soul arises as the feelings find a sympathetic and compassionate link to nature, life and others. The soul bears the stamp of experience, and experience individuates us, makes us unique. Like cars rolling off the assembly line that all may seem to be the same, we each become different as we encounter different experiences and environments. Some cars may be taken care of, even loved, others neglected, and each bears the marks of its experience. As our soul individuates and becomes unique we begin to find our own direction in life, particularly when we assume control of our own nature and energy.

So why does the devil want our soul? Demons don't really want our souls, they just don't want us to have souls because having a soul disinclines one to act like a soulless being, or what is referred to currently as a person suffering from anti-social personality disorder, more commonly called a sociopath or a psychopath. The more soulful we become, the more we come to care about our others.

Spirit

Our nature, as we've said, is essentially energetic. Some people when they talk of spirit, mean spiritual. But we mean spirit as in spirited, as in team spirit. It is associated often with courage, but it may also be associated with one's attitude and personality, although the Spirit isn't so much the personality as manifesting through personality. In a higher sense, however, it is the energy that composes our being, and we are composed of pure energy, and the direction it follows as it individuates and finds its place, ... or more accurately, not place, but direction in the Universe. The more we become our true s'elves the greater our spirit becomes. Those who have lost their spirit become depressed, have no will to live and often just die. Spirit then is the Will to Be. It is our Life Force and it is the integrating aspect of our being. When it departs the body with its soul the body disintegrates. It is Spirit that Arose into Being toward individuation from the pure undifferentiated energy that is also pure consciousness that is the Source of All things in the Universe.

The goal of life is to unite once again with the pure energy and consciousness in an individuated fashion so the whole Universe will be conscious and aware of its'elf and each and every part thereof conscious of its'elf in harmony, which is to say love, with the all of life forever. This is the union of the soul and the spirit.

However, we don't ask you to believe this, only to consider it and decide for yours'elf, based upon your own knowledge and experience, what the truth is for you.

The Lessons of the Soul

Each of us have lessons we need to learn in our lives. Our parents, or other well meaning individuals, often try to tell us things or give us hints that will help us avoid the mistakes they feel they made in their own lives, but unless we have, in fact, mastered these lessons in a previous life, it is most likely that we will repeat those mistakes until we master them our own s'elves that is to say develop this mastery as an established part of our own soul.

It is said that those who ignore history are doomed to repeat it, and this is certainly true, and this is the case often on a large scale of the above stated principle. Until we as individuals, or as a society overall, master certain mistakes, we will repeat them endlessly. This is a function of karma, which is also a manifestation of ignorance. Until we learn how to do things better, we will continue to do them in inferior, which is to say less effective and usually more painful, ways.

Thus as much as we may wish to help others by giving them advice, this is seldom helpful. Those who don't seek our advice do not value our advice and guidance, or even wisdom when offered to them. Alas, these elves have often found that even those who do seek our advice are less than likely to follow it. Again, the individual's habits of being draw them back into repetitive and often erroneous efforts, and this will continue until the individual finally dedicates hirs'elf to the upliftment of hir soul/spirit, and this sHe alone can do for hirs'elf. These elves do not despair when another fails to heed our advice, we have come to understand that each needs to find hir own way in hir own time, and we are at peace within ours'elves with that fact. Our own challenges and struggles are elsewhere.

And while there is wisdom in the world that can help uplift it, each individual still must realize that wisdom within hir own soul. This is why in society most of the individuals can be quite tolerant toward racial integration, for example, and there will still be a minority of individuals who are hateful and prejudiced against other races. Even the weight of peer pressure from the mass of society will not transform an individual until the individual embraces and realizes that greater understanding and acceptance in hir own s'elf. Try as we might, we simply can't force people to change for the better, anymore than we can use force to make people love and respect us.

From this reality two things follow, the first is that whatever lessons are offered must be suited to the nature and level of the individual seeking enlightenment. Thus while an aspiring elfin can learn from this, or our other books, only those of a certain level and readiness will be attracted to these offerings, and each will derive from them what they are ready to receive at this time. This is in part why two individuals can read the same book, or see the same movie, and one will think it is the greatest thing sHe has ever encountered and the other will find it totally incomprehensible and worthless.

The other important element is that the lessons offered must be geared toward the time, culture and society as it is currently manifesting. Everything must be updated in time, as we expect this book will be by other elves, or by our own s'elves in other bodies, far in the future. At the same time, we are ever called to sort out what is a temporary manifestation from the enduring and eternal. We teach for our time, but those things of which we hint are aspects of our immortality. We seek beyond the illusion, the maya, or seeming-ness of life, to the underlying principles that compose life and have meaning for us not simply in this particular lifetime but for the eternal life of our spirit/soul.

And thus we must speak of the first things, the Source from which all springs.

Being and Non-Being

There are two basic states in the Universe: Being and Non-Being. Non-Being by its nature doesn't exist. That is its nature. And thus there is only Being, which is, always has been, and always will be in an Eternal Now. It might be conceived of as energy, energy that can neither be created nor destroyed. It is pure in its nature, that is to say utterly undifferentiated, and absolutely protean, it can become anything possible and will become everything that can be, all at the same time, which is always Now.

There is not a single force or God beyond Being, Being bears the potential of the Divine within its nature and this Divinity or perfection ever seeks to come into Being, that is to manifest. And yet, Being is already Perfect within its'elf. It is a paradox. When you understand this in your inner being, you will have solved one of the great mysteries of the Universe, be at one with yours'elf, and the all of Life.

Since Being is All, and all things come into being simultaneous, the Universe springs (an important word that, for in Elven Mythology all life comes from the Sacred Spring) into manifestation. However, since all things possible come into being, the possibility of differentiation also arises. Not all things can be at the same time in the same place. This creates dimensions of being or manifestation that instantly spread out into Space. But what is Space? Space is Non-Being that paradoxically both exists and doesn't exists and thus allows Being to spread through it. It is also Time as we normally conceive it. In the Qabalah, this would be expressed as Ein (Ayn) Soph, Divine Being and Ein (infinite nothingness). Every possibility strives to realize itself, which is to say it hungers for its perfection. In a way you could say that Being, in its purity is the Divine Father, although we elves call it the Magic, or the Miraculous. Non-Being in its purity is the Divine Mother, it is the womb in which the Universe gestates as it grows, evolves toward its Perfected Realization. In another sense however, it is the absent God. It is the Divine that removed itself so we could Be. It is sometimes thought of as deus otiosus, or deus absconditus, the idle or hidden god that has retired from its creation. It is not, so we may be, and yet it lives within us. And as we say, we elves call it Magic.

Conscious and Un-Conscious

This paradoxical relationship between Being and Non-Being is reflected in the Conscious and the Unconscious. It is also reflected in the aspect of Life and Death. If we are Unconscious do we exist? Well, we'd tend to say yes, since each night most of us sleep, and are thus unconscious and yet continue to exist, or assume we did when we awaken. This is similar to the question: if the tree falls in the forest and no one is around to hear it, does it make any sound? Sleep is unconsciousness, and unconsciousness is in a sense Non-Being. It is and isn't at the same time. It is the little death. Consciousness is then Being. And adepts and yogis strive toward continuity of consciousness, that is to say they seek to achieve consciousness even when the body sleeps, even when the body dissolves. For we come back to the question: are we really alive if we don't know we are alive? Observing people in comas we could say yes. But then the question is, are they really living? Alive as a body, yes. But alive as a spirit, soul and consciousness?

Pure Awareness

What most people call consciousness is an awareness of their thoughts, beliefs and ideas. In the animal kingdom, consciousness is an instinctual awareness and lacks, for the most part, the beliefs, ideas and self-concepts found among humans. In the human being, the idea driven consciousness comes to fore but, as we've pointed out already, this is primarily directed and motivated by ideas ruled by our passions and emotionally connected ideas. We think ours'elves to be free but really our lives are controlled by these passions and beliefs.

When we are born into a particular life we come bearing the imprint on our souls of our pervious experiences. Obviously, when we are reborn we don't have the same body. So our bodies, as they currently exist, clearly are not a part of our immortal s'elf, although they are composed of the energy that is, in its'elf, immortal. We are mostly formed from Star-stuff or Stardust, and elves are particularly aware of this fact. So when we come into a new life, our soul/spirit gathers around it the available stardust/energy to form a new body.

Since this stardust also bears the imprint of its past, in the form of a DNA coding directive, we also come into each life with a racial consciousness, formed in what is often called the Collective Unconscious. We also have a human consciousness, and bear the imprint of our evolution through various forms from all our previous incarnations. To become truly immortal beings, that is to say, immortal in the way that vampires are seen as being immortal, having a permanent immortal physical body, we need to integrate our consciousness with and merge with the consciousness of the energy that temporarily composes us. Of course, elves are often also seen as being Immortal, particularly in our more ephemeral forms, or our ethereal or etheric bodies combined with our astral bodies.

In time our bodies will become more resilient, less physical, and more like light, thus more ephemeral. The dimensions we will reside within, the dimension of Elfin/Faerie will be similar to living in a dream. We will have greater powers, such as the power to fly, and the ability to do things that we can now only dream of doing. And yet it will be every bit as real as a dream seems when we are in it, or every bit as real as this illusionary world that we currently abide within.

Also, just as clearly when we pass from one body to another, we don't carry our thoughts, feelings and beliefs with us, or our memories, unless indeed we have obtained continuity of consciousness and have born our mind through the death process, which, honestly, these particular elves are nowhere near to achieving. Are you? If you are, you will be able to tell because you will be able to remain aware throughout the night as your body sleeps without losing consciousness. Sleep, as we said, is the little death. It is the reflection in microcosm, As Above/So Below, As Within/So Without, of the life death cycle.

For most individuals, the death experience and the assumption of a new stardust body is like suffering from total amnesia. You don't remember anything. You don't even know what you know. For instance, in amnesia, you may know how to type or play a piano, but you don't know that you know how to do it until you sit down at a typewriter, or computer, or piano and suddenly find that typing or playing piano comes automatically to you. So, too, in moving from one life to another, we carry certain abilities with us. We don't necessarily know that we know, rather we feel we were born with certain talents and abilities, and indeed we were. Usually, we find we learn these things very quickly and easily. These skills seem to come naturally to us.

Our feelings, not so much our emotions, but mostly our feelings, because they are by their nature essentially unconscious, come easily through the transitional state of death. We may not remember whom we loved or liked or disliked, but if we encounter them again or someone like them we immediately sense our attraction, or our repulsion. There are certain individuals that we know immediately even though it seems we have never met them previously. So until we are able to carry our memories from life to life consciously, they are still born in our soul, particularly those things that are most important to us, which is love and relationship, as well as having an instinctual recognition of and attraction to those with whom we have a karmic connection either positive or negative.

We can see this fact reflected in our current life in our conscious and unconscious. The basic consciousness is everything of which we are currently aware. But we also have an unconscious which composes everything of which we are not aware, which for most of us is far vaster than our conscious awareness. Consider all the things we don't know, and add to it all the things, events, facts, people, experiences we have forgotten, which are stored in our brains but which, for most of them, are lost to us except at certain times. So, too, are our experiences stored in our soul, but only accessible under certain profound circumstances, although occasionally brought to mind by our encounters in the world, just as memories may be brought back into consciousness by a particular, song, smell, or experience. Our soul stores all our experiences and in that way is linked to the Akashic record, which records all experiences of all beings. The Akashic record is the library of the Soul of the Universe.

The Witnesses

Occult or esoteric teachings tell us there are three aspects of consciousness in the human being. The first, as we've explained, is the automatic, or robotic consciousness. In its simplest from it regulates the body, In its higher form, it develops mental facilities that, for the most part, are unaware of the automatic and instinctual activity of the body awareness. However, this aspect is only a more developed form of the automatic system and is, itself, controlled by beliefs, passions and instinctual drives toward survival/success and pleasure/success. Most human beings are controlled by outside forces, the interplay of the dominant interacting forces of their social environment.

However there are, we are told, two witnesses to the actions of this intelligent robotic being. One is called the Permanent Witness, but which these elves call the Spirit Witness, and the other the Spiritual Witness or as we call it the Soulful Witness, and this is the Higher or Perfect S'elf, the True S'elf. One has a personal quality to it and the other, impersonal, that is to say it sees beyond our current sense of individuality.

The Spirit Witness bears our individual nature through manifestations. Its consciousness is deeper than the surface consciousness that most of us associate with our minds and our reasoning facility. It is more feeling in nature and it tends to communicate with us through our dreams. (Note that feelings are usually associated with the Soul, however, it is important to understand we have divided the Spirit and Soul merely to examine them. They are actually two aspects of one being and thus naturally share certain properties.) It is associated with the development of our personality, our sense of s'elf hood. It bears witness to us as we progress from one life to another, and in that way is immortal. However, it still has a sense of separateness about it, and as yet it hasn't fully understood its connection to the whole of life.

The True S'elf that witnesses us is our Higher, or really, Perfected S'elf. It is in many ways the Divine Potentiality that calls to us and toward which we evolve through becoming and manifestation. At the same time, it always is and will be, and we are always that Perfected Being, but are in the process of Realizing it, both becoming conscious of its being, and making it real. The Egyptians called this the Ka of our being and it is this being, which is ours'elves perfected, that sounds our True Name, which is the vibrational sound our Perfected Being makes, and which calls to us as we endeavor to harmonize our temporary being with this greater, purer, sound. It is this energy or aspect of our being that seeks to perfect us, and to integrate our consciousness and our soulful nature with the stardust that we use to manifest, so we may become truly immortal in a permanent fashion. This aspect, however, tends to be impersonal since it is not attached to the current manifestation of our personality, nor to the current manifestation of our soul. It seeks to unite us with the all of life in its Divine Manifestation and will do whatever necessary to accomplish this end. We might call this aspect of ours'elves our Immortal Conscious Happiness. It is aware, that is it bears the memory or imprint of being part of the One.

The Spirit seeks to develop us as individuals, the Soul seeks to connect and unite us with the All; although, it may be also said that the Soul is our means of connecting and uniting with the All. It may seem that these two are in conflict, and in fact, in a sense they are because they tend in what seems on the surface to be opposite directions. The Spirit pushes us to perfect ours'elves, to become truly individuated, while the Soul seeks to unite us with all others. In the minds of most people these would seem to be opposing tendencies, one separative and the other hungering for union. But as we continue, we will see that this seeming opposition is an illusion, just as two sides of a coin are still one coin.

Soul Mates and Soul Bonds

Most people are aware of the idea of a Soul Mate, that is a person one is linked with in one's soul and with whom one is destined to unite. In the otherkin community there is also the idea of a Soul Bond, a similar link, that is two or more individuals destined to be together, however, not necessarily for romantic purposes, as the Soul Mate usually connotes, but coming together to help each other on their spiritual path, or as we elves call it the Path of Elfin, and the journey of the evolutionary quest. Both of these are inspired by the Soulful Witness, which seeks to unite us with, or help us to realize our unity with others. The Soul Mate aspect especially has this energy because, while romantic, it tends to often indicate those who are so close together that they function and become almost like one person. In fact in the experience of these elves, most people who have been together for any length of time do tend to become very like each other.

This Soul Mate union can become so strong, that is the individuals can merge so deeply, that in some cases in future lives the individuals can inhabit one body becoming a greater individual. There are some, we know, who will immediately bulk at this idea, fearing to loose their individuality, but you should know that this union is almost never forced. It happens because these individuals love each other so deeply that they hunger for greater union and merge together. They, in a sense, crawl into each other's soul. This merging can also be seen in the hunger by mystics and certain religious devotees to be filled with the ecstatic love of their chosen "god".

Curiously, this can never happen among or between individuals who are not strong individuals. It is true that some will look upon such individuals as being weak for yielding their individuality so easily, but in fact having achieved all they wished, or needed to achieve as individuals, they then seek a greater, more powerful union based upon love. They lose their s'elves in their other. They still are and yet they are more.

Perhaps this can be seen in what is called multiple personality disorder where the individual encounters so much stress that it breaks again into two or more personalities in an attempt to shield the primary personal, the union, from harm. The therapists dealing with such an individual seek to re-integrate the personalities into one being again.

The Soul Bond tends to have a similar energy, but one that preserves the integrity of each soul/spirit participating in the union. This bond provides mutual assistance for developing spirits. This is along the lines of what the Buddhist might call Right Association, that is to say hanging out with others who are also on the Path.

Again, no one, or any power, forces you together with other souls into one being, or if it does so, it almost never lasts. True union is based on Love. In fact it occurs because the love is so deeply felt that the beings merge. It is an effect of True Love.

As we've said, the All of Life, is destined to be consciously aware. That is every atom in the Universe, every atom in one's body will become conscious. But you can see that without a sense of cooperative union such a system would very quickly disintegrate into its most elemental parts. We are draw together through attraction. And just like sex draws us together, and offers us pleasure in exchange for union, the Universe, the Divine, the Magic makes our merging worth our while with ecstatic bliss.

And yet while we share a body, the body of the Cosmic Soul/Spirit, we are still uniquely ours'elves, just as the cells in our body are each differentiated. Our heart is not our liver, nor our lungs, our spleen. If we were exactly the same in union, we'd dissolve into a blob. Fear not, the Magic didn't make you unique in order to destroy your uniqueness. Rather it seeks to makes us so we fit perfectly together. The Universe is a puzzle being put together. However, it is a Magic Puzzle whose image continues to change. We might call it a motion picture puzzle.

So how does one retain one's individuality while being conscious of the whole? By becoming increasingly aware of one's unconscious elements, which include not only all we have known and experienced and forgotten, but also the Collective Unconsciousness of our genetic line, our race, and humanity over all as well as the all of life. In other words, we come into psychic and intuitive contact with everything that seems separate or beyond us. Just as our eyes capture light from around us and translate it into images of the dimensions in our immediate vicinity so, too, do our feelings, via intuition and psychic perception, pick up the signals from all things that are in our vicinity. And all things are connected in the Universe. Anything that is not connected in this Universe does not exist for us. Also, Quantum Physics tells us that any two things that have ever come into contact have an immediate psychic rapport no matter how long or far the time or space (really the same thing) separating them. Some folks refer to this extension of the Spirit through the Soul as the Expansion of Consciousness.

This psychic harmony brings us into rapport with a wider range of life and yet does not violate nor dissolve the essential unity of our individual nature. And while many people believe that humans, along with higher beings, such as angels, are the only ones who have individual nature, we elves do not accept this idea. It is clear to us that animals, while often having less opportunity to develop their uniqueness, and while more powerfully directed by their drives, still have personalities and individual natures. They are also unique beings, just as no tree or plant is exactly the same although they continue to conform to the limitations and variations of their species.

Ultimately, as we evolve we will each become totally unique; we will become Singularities, while being ever more in harmony with the all of life. However, true immortality will not come to us until we are s'elf sufficient, that is to say we will no longer need to consume outside of ours'elves to live but will generate the very energy we survive upon. We will be complete symbiotic beings, feeding each other with love as we live together in love forever.

Vegetarianism

Among the otherkin and Elfae communities there is no topic that is more likely to arouse intense conflict than the issue of eating or not eating meat. As we said in the previous section, the more we evolve the less we will be dependent upon gross sources of food, particularly food/energy that is obtained by force and violence. There are however individuals who are not ready to give up meat eating, and there are those who tell us that their bodies require it. We don't argue with them. If they need it, or if they wish to eat it, that is their business. We are not here to convert anyone to vegetarianism, or any of our other views. However, the fact remains as we become more evolved we will be ever less depended upon gross forms of nourishment, and as we become more soulfully aware we will become ever less inclined toward killing other beings to live. We would no more kill an animal than we'd chop off our own foot and eat it. Although, in another sense the Ouroboros worm swallowing its own tail tells us that is exactly what we will do; we will consume the energy we create and be continually s'elf generating.

Again, soulful evolution is voluntary in nature. Such higher merging is nearly always based upon love and depends not only on the individual's willingness to participate, but hir concerted effort to do so. One must want to advance as a Soulful Spirit and actively seek to progress. It does one no good to give up eating meat if they don't really wish to do so. Intention is a vital aspect of Magic. In the future, we will live on love. We will, in a sense, swallow each other.

The Rationalizing Mind

The higher robotic thinking mind, while an evolutionary development over animal instinctual behavior, is non-the-less a barrier to higher consciousness. A barrier is also created between us, and the instinctual awareness, which is an aspect of animal nature that includes the instinctual awareness of early humanoid beings such as our Paleolithic ancestors. This, however, is an intermediate phase, and while we elves often mourn the loss of these instincts, and of atrophied senses such as heighten awareness of smells, many of these instinctual senses will return to us in a greater and an improved fashion as we develop our soulful intuitive psychic connection with the all of life. We are, in a way, moving away from physical senses, just as we are evolving beyond a gross physical body, to more subtle perceptions that will be even keener than those we currently have.

However, in coming to realize, that is make real, which is to say not simply mentally understand, that we are unique beings, we also understand that all of the Universe, every bit of it, is unique. Every being is unique and all of us are the same in that we are each unique, as well as being composed of the same essential energy, which is to say, the Magic.

The process of this development is through the Spirit, or the urge toward S'elf Realization, gaining ascendency over the Robotic or Instinctual s'elf, while in as much as possible retaining instinctual awareness. We thus gain power over our own s'elves and from this comes increasing power to guide and direct our lives, rather than being pushed around endlessly by our unthinking reactions. However, even greater power comes to us as our Soulful nature rises into ascendency and we increase our connection to elements that seemed separate from us. Remember, we can't influence anything with which we have no connection. This soulful consciousness lifts us from separative or ego awareness, which has been thoroughly established, into a unitive awareness with life, nature, and the realms of magic that we call Elfin/Faerie. This connectivity heightens our senses and gives us access psychically to information that would previously have been inaccessible to us. The Veil is parted, the mysteries revealed, and as it is often said, "Knowledge is Power." The Knowledge of Elfin is Magical Power.

To become one's true s'elf, is ultimately to become one with Elfin. We sense the Realm as the Realm senses us. As the ancient formula goes, the King and the Land are one, and all elves are royal beings. We are each and every one of us a part of Elfin/Faerie, which is not a land so much as a Magic that lives within and through us. It is a state of being, a state of consciousness.

The Quest

The quest is to become one's true s'elf and to live in the Realms of Elfin/Faerie in Love and Happiness Forever, in others words to Live Happily Ever After. This involves the evolution of the s'elf into the supra-dimensional realms where the Shining Ones abide, those beings of light who are our ancestors and who have passed through every stage of evolution, just as we are doing, to gain that realm of being and realization where all is radiant light. This is achieved by uniting our spirit, our sense of s'elfhood, with our soul, our sense of union with the Magic and the All of Life.

We should remember that our Soul is already immortal. It is the light, or energy, or Magic that we use to create our beings. It remembers always, in the nature of its being, its Oneness with the Source, which is the Divine Magic. By integrating our sense of s'elf with this soulful essence, we become immortal as individuals, and yet at the same time we realize our union with the Magic in doing so. This involves the illumination of our bodies as well as our minds. Our bodies and our minds become filled with light. We become Radiant beings.

This involves the conscious development of the Body of Light, the inner energetic body around which our apparent physical body is congealed. As we develop this body of light, and instill it with our spirit, it will become an immortal body, that is to say the immortal aspect of the light will merge, as our souls merge, into a cohesive union that will not dissolve in the way that our gross physical body dissolves causing what is typically called death, or which we might see as a divorce between our consciousness and the energy that temporarily composed our body.

To achieve this goal, we need first of all to master our s'elves and rise above robotic behavior and reactions. However, this is not to say we will not have what appear to be automatic functions. In fact, the more we come into control over our own s'elves and the more integrated we are as s'elves, the more we will rely on our sub-parts to rule their own s'elves effectively for the benefit of the whole. So in essence, we are not so much assuming control over every aspect of our being as purifying our being so we may effectively delegate our authority. To a great extent, this means ridding ours'elves of bad habits and destructive behaviors while allowing those things that are essentially harmless to continue. We need to remember our bodies have needs also, which if denied for too long will cause rebellion in our being. A body that suffers austerity for too long will revolt. Yet, at the same time we cannot let the body rule us to the point where we lose control over it, thus we train it to function perfectly. We take great care of it and see that all its needs are met in a positive way. If we do that, it will for the most part take care of itself leaving us free to pursue our higher quest.

For the mass of humanity at this point in evolution, this quest is not even possible in a conscious fashion, although all beings are on the Path of Evolutionary Development whether they realize it or not. They are driven by their mental percepts, and are ruled by their notions of religious and moral behavior and their urges to violate these rules according to their desires, passions and selfish interest. They cannot, however, function in the higher realms of moral ambiguity where decisions of right and wrong are not based upon strict rules of behavior espoused by a particular religion or social group, but by the nuances of the circumstances that confront one, and a higher sense of what is right for ones'elf and all others. (Do an Internet search for Lawrence Kohlberg's *stages of moral development* for more on this.)

However, elves and other aspiring adepts feel a constant appeal by our higher natures to consider not just ours'elves, or even our social group, race, nation, etc. but the concerns of humanity as a whole. Note, however, that concern for one's family, social group, race, nation and such are an intermediate step that leads one beyond mere selfish interest and is a good thing, although limited, and thus these allegiances beyond the s'elf often create tragic consequences as seen in holy wars and other conflicts between separative groups.

If the Spirit manifests without the Call of the Soul, it seeks to control the lower s'elf and the automatic impulses, but does not have the influence of that loving and unitive soulful nature. It follows a Will to Power, but purely from the urge to uplift the s'elf uncaring of the needs or concerns of others. When this happens there is a tendency for the individual to manifest, at least for a time, as a Dark Lodge Magician/Sorcerer ever vying for mastery over the lower nature and over other individuals. The individual seeks mastery through domination. This, however, is always an intermediate state and one can never rise to the highest realms of manifestation, or enter the inner circle of Elfin, unless one evolves beyond this stage of development.

It is not that there are not aspects for cooperative action on this level. As we've pointed out, Dark Sorcerers often form an uneasy bond for mutual benefit, but the moment the bond violates the s'elf interest of one of its members, or an individual feels sHe can gain more without the group or without a particular member of the group, or vice versa, that bond instantly dissolves, this divorce quite often being accompanied by betrayal, treachery and murder.

If one feels the call of the Soul, one becomes overwhelmed with an intense need to unite with higher power. If this happens without the influence of the Spirit it appears, as it so often does in religious devotees, as the intense hunger for union with the Divine. This is also the situation for Mystics. This calling is often faked by those in prison, who suddenly convert to Christianity, etc. to show a change of heart and receive preferable consideration at their parole hearing. However, it surely happens in a genuine fashion as well when the individual is overwhelmed by sympathy for those they've harmed, and guilt about the harm they have caused to others. This is often brought about by their own suffering, which helps the individual discover compassion for those who also have suffered. This personal understanding of suffering thus arouses the hidden soulful nature. Frequently in these circumstances, the individual sees hir individual nature, or ego, as being bad or evil or the source of hir problem, and thus seeks to abnegate it to rise to a higher level of realization. They often feel that they cannot truly progress without subjugating the separative ego that lead them into trouble in the first place.

The alternative, of course, is the cooperative action of the Spirit and the Soul, which is the preferred path for Elfae. The interaction of these forces initiates the Alchemical process that leads to the Alchemical Marriage. It would be a mistake to think that this takes place in realms beyond us. The intermingling of these two, their courtship and romance, so to speak, come about within our beings. The Way into Elfin is always an interior one. Just as our success in the world depends upon Mastering our own being so, too, the gateway to Faerie is to be found within our own souls. Thus the way out is in, and the way in is out. This is to say, to transform the world we must first master our own s'elves, but to transform ours'elves we must also master our actions and behaviors, which is to say our Magic, in the world. We must look to the effects of our actions and become increasingly aware of them.

Some people view this interaction, this romance, between the spirit and the soul as a conflict between competing interests, each striving to gain ascendancy. But then, some people also view courtship in the same way. However, we elves, for the most part, like our romance less stormy and more filled with delight, and we integrate our soulful natures and our spirits in the same fashion. We view it not as a game for ascendancy of one aspect of being over the other, but a dance that requires cooperation from both parties to be truly harmonious and beautiful.

We can only realize our immortality, our Divine Magical nature, by realizing it within ours'elves. Seeing it beyond us ever keeps it separate from us. It is only by realizing it within, by becoming one with it that our own Divinity Manifests. However, our Spirit alone cannot achieve this. For to be Divine alone is to be separate from the rest of creation, which isn't Divine at all. Divinity is found in Love, in being ours'elves in harmony with the Divine Magic.

It is said in the Bible that, "in the beginning was the word and the word was with God, and the word was God." That word is a Word of Power, a magical word. It is the vibration and frequency that is your true name, the magic of your being, and your true destiny as a soulful spirit.

The energy that composes your body is from the Source, the Divine Magic, and it remembers it in its own nature. It may seem solid, but it is in fact, starlight and as we become ever more aware of that fact, we awaken to our true s'elves and find our way to the center of the Elfin where we will discover our beloved kindred awaiting us.

The Courtship

Until we indeed rise to the higher levels of realization it is difficult to truly grasp the nature of the Soul and the Spirit, although the Soul is in its way simpler and more easily grasped than the Spirit. Its urge is always toward Union, while the Spirit seeks success through differentiation, which by its nature is different for each being. However, we might look at both of these by extending the ideas of the heart and the mind. We could call the Soul heartfelt intelligence or unitive intelligence and the Spirit Mindful intelligence or perhaps discriminative intelligence for it ever seeks to define what is and isn't the s'elf.

The awakening of the Soul involves the activation of the fourth or heart Chakra, which reaches out to link us to others via sympathy and compassion. It is the movement of the Drive toward Eternal Happiness that has evolved from mere satisfaction of the pleasure impulse to an understanding of the interrelationship and commonality of all life as it strives toward realization. This is the first real impulse beyond the isolated s'elf and it is the first step upward toward higher realization.

This reaching out, so to speak, is met in turn by the soul nature of others who are reaching as well, so it is, in a sense immediately rewarded, although not always so on the material plane. This is to say that esoterically it finds response in the Universe both from others who are seeking union and even more so from the Soul Nature of the Universe that ever promotes harmony among its constituent parts, although no individual in one's immediate environment will necessarily respond to this impulse in a material or observable fashion, although that possibility is not precluded.

This response from the Universe and others reaching out has an immediate effect when it is perceived as reassuring the individual, soothing the individual's doubts, and letting the individuated s'elf know that it is not alone in the Universe, as it comes to believe it might be during the Dark Night of the Soul; and that there are others, and other powers out there, that will aid and support one in one's quest for realization. In other words, the Magic responds and by its nature its response is Magical. For those of a religious or mystical nature, one feels the Presence of the Divine. For elves this primarily manifests as an understanding that one's true elfin kin, as well as Elfin itself, are ever there for us, sending us magic to help and guide us.

Some think of this Soulful intelligence as being Impersonal; however, we elves tend to see it as transpersonal, supra-personal, or even ultra-personal. It is very personal but not in any exclusive sense. It ever seeks to unite the elf with others, and it ever seeks to unite all life into a harmonious marriage of ecstatic being. It is not clinical, as some seem to imagine in calling it impersonal, but quite the opposite; it is deeply and profoundly intimate. For intimacy is its goal, and its nature.

The other force of realization, or the other dancer in this supra-personal courtship, is the Spirit, which having gained ascendency over the primary instincts and impulses, seeks to understand and define its'elf, as well as fulfill its'elf to its greatest extent. It strives ever toward Mastery, Adeptship, and the realization of its Divine Nature, which is to say it seeks

God-dess-hood. It seeks to create and to have absolute Mastery over its own life. It seeks the power to control its'elf and its life, and thus choose and guide its Destiny.

It should be understood that all aspects that do not belong in their essence to either of these forces is transitory and thus mortal; although in a sense all things are immortal in their essence, that is to say in the energy that composes them; but some things are only passing through us or us them, such as opinions, thoughts, ideas, emotions, and the energy we use to create our bodies. We are ever seeking our own true s'elves, or our true configuration of being, and until we find this, until that transformation occurs we are ever in a marriage of convenience with the energy that composes us.

The Dancers

As we said, there are two essential energies or intelligences that are involved in this Dance of Life and Liberation. We say two, because they have different impulses, but it is important to understand that while we look at them as being two and as being distinct for convenience, ultimately they are One. They are destined to be together, united forever by love.

However, to understand them more clearly, let us look at the aspects that differentiate them.

The Spirit, in union with the body's genetic directives ever seeks to:

1. Perpetuate its existence and to do so as it currently conceives it, which is to say as it understands life on this planet at this time.
2. It thus seeks success within the world as it exists and as it understands it to be.

3. However, to do this it is called to find a balance between its impulse to individualize, to be unique, and its hunger for acceptance. It is driven ever to make a choice between freedom and acceptance, and in most cases this involves a compromise, some people choosing conformity and thus acceptance over freedom, and some choosing freedom, that is control over their own responses over acceptance, but few chose one without at least a bit of the other. It needs to be understood that the impulse to conform to gain acceptance is in part inspired by the higher aspects of the Soul that ever seeks union, but it is also a function of survival urge and a drive for success in the world, which is promoted by the spirit.
4. Because it seeks success of the s'elf in the world as it currently conceives it, it also continues to view the world from that perspective. Thus the pure egotism of the spirit stymies our advance toward higher realization, for by itself it never thinks beyond itself.
5. To ascend beyond our current state, we need information and energy from beyond ours'elves. We may look within, but as we've indicated, within is the gateway to the beyond. And this brings us inevitably to the Soul.

The Soul intelligence in contrast ever seeks to:
1. Unite with the Spirit, which it loves and adores and wants what it wants, but from a higher perspective and with an eye always toward an even greater union.
2. It desires to make this union permanent, thus immortal, which is also a drive of the Spirit.
3. Thus it views things concerning the individual, the spirit, from the point of view of immortality. It sees what is

eternal in the individual, and ever promotes those aspects of its being.
4. The effect of this is to ever open the Spirit to sympathetic and compassionate association with all of life, for this is the key to higher knowledge, and to wisdom attained through intuitive association.
5. It is therefore also passionate in its nature as a person in love is passionate and consumed with the sense of its beloved, unlike the Spirit that tends to calculate (Note, however, that when the Spirit is Soulful it can also be quite passionate, and it is in this way that it inspires others). It seeks to overcome all obstacles though the immensity of its feeling, and to wash away all doubts with ecstatic revelation. In the lower reaches this can be observed in those who think they will win the subject of their infatuation over if the individual just realized how much they love them.
6. It sees no blemishes. To the Soulful intelligence the beloved is essentially perfect, with one or two minor changes that association with it will naturally bring about.
7. It believes that Love is the greatest power, the panacea that will cure all ills and overcome all obstacles.
8. It loves for love's sake. It has no ulterior motives other than to love and uplift the subject of its love.
9. Its love is ever expansive and overflowing. Unlike the lower impulses of this energy that seek to possess in an exclusive fashion, the highest aspect ever seeks greater union with the all of life that it knows, like its'elf, to be Divine. Thus it ever seeks greater, wider, and more expansive union. The love of humanity, the love of animals, the love of the planet, the love of the stars, the love of life eternally.

The Ego

When most people speak of the ego, particularly those following a spiritual path, they mean an overinflated sense of the s'elf and a dominating self-interest. The ego in this sense is seen as a negative function that needs to be limited or eliminated. Psychologists, however, speak of Ego-strength, meaning a positive sense of one's s'elfhood that helps protect one from depression and the vicissitudes of life in the world.

That first form of the ego is a function of the lower self, the robotic self, and this can be seen in how fragile, sensitive and easily insulted, and thus easily manipulated it is. This ego is reactionary and it acts in an attempt to protect the personality from outside incursions, and to establish the higher sense of ego that constitutes ego-strength. Because it is essentially weak and born of insecurity, it tends to overcompensate for its feelings of inadequacy.

As this ego evolves, that is to say as the Spirit gains more control of the robotic-pure animal impulses, it becomes less fragile, and thus less likely to be offended, and therefore less easily manipulated; but without the influence of the Soul it becomes simply selfish and self serving. It is more powerful and more secure than the lower ego, but still ever protecting its'elf from potential attacks from outside forces. While it is less likely to be manipulated, it still bears a great deal of paranoia.

Ego-strength, however, arises from this higher, although often still selfish level of being, and it is ego-strength that allows us to interact with others without, or with less, fear, and thus makes union and cooperation easier. The stronger the individual is within hir own s'elf, the greater hir capacity for uniting with others.

It should be noted that we ascend, that is to say evolve, in great part by becoming more. Thus we are constantly integrating the various parts of ours'elves, which also means the various personalities into a whole. And as we've pointed out, at times of great pressure that the whole can fragment into the constituent personalities in order to protect itself.

Each of these personalities have their own ego drive and at times compete with each other until the overriding power of the Spirit under the influence of the Soul brings them to a place where they can merge to the benefit of all. This understanding, that what is best for the whole is also good for the parts, is an essential realization of the higher nature. This is commonly expressed in the idea that the individual should sacrifice hir own exclusive interests for that of the greater good; however, this idea is so often evoked by Dark Sorcerers and Petty Sorcerers to obtain their own will that such urges to sacrifice must be analyzed carefully. Often one is being called to sacrifice not for the greater good but for the will to power of a few sorcerers who, while Petty Sorcerers, are still quite adept at what they do. On the other hand, in all cases where such sacrifice is genuine, the individual ascends by uniting with hir soulful nature.

Defining the S'elf

The Spirit urges us to become fully ours'elves. To do this we gain control of our passions and our drives and we rid ours'elves of all that is inferior in our character. Our actions are magic, that is to say they have effects, karma, and we may denounce within ours'elves things we've done in our past that we are not proud of doing, or that we regret, and we may change ours'elves, that is re-define ours'elves, not only intellectually, but by our actions, by ceasing to act in a particular way and no longer putting energy toward those modes of being.

However, we must also accept what we have done in order to accomplish this. We must admit our wrongs, and also make amends, as is advised in AA and 12 step programs. This making amends and the suffering through the karmic results of our actions clears us from these actions of the past, and while we must still, at least in a particular lifetime acknowledge them, this cleansing of karma in coordination with our efforts to cease creating that karma, alters our character. Thus we define ours'elves not by what we think about ours'elves, or what we say about ours'elves, but by our actions, which is to say our Magic. We shape our lives, our future, through what we do. In that sense, we are our Magic.

It is said that Thoughts are Things, and this is true, but on the level of development that most of humanity is upon at this time, thoughts are mostly important in that they lead to action/magic. What we think does not instantly come to be. And it is a good thing that this is so, for the thinking processes of most of us are too chaotic for this to be the case. We would very quickly destroy ours'elves. (Instead of doing so relatively slowly as is humanity's current case.) However, as we gain increasing control over our beings, and our consciousness and thoughts, our thoughts will become actions/magic and take effect near instantaneously. This is still far, far in the future, however, and need not concern us now except to know that this is the direction toward which we evolving. We will have to have much greater Mastery over our beings before this level of development will occur, both in terms of our ability and our safety.

We need to note that what we think to be ours'elves, what we feel to be ours'elves, and the ways we define our s'elves, are continually changing and evolving. Much of what we think or feel about ours'elves comes from others. We are defined by our interactions with the outside world, and the people we encounter in it. This is a function of the Soul, but most often of a lower nature. By this we mean that those who offer us opinions and reactions to us always do so from their own level of development, which is usually from the robotic self or the lower Spirit. However, our own Spirit can be seen in what we accept or reject. We are in many ways shaped and defined by our environments, but not all beings are shaped, or react, in the same way by the similar circumstances. Our own spirit, and our karma, has a great influence on how much we accept or reject from the influence of our environment. Our Spirit effects our power to resist, bounce back, or overcome circumstance, while our karma affects how much help, or how many opportunities, might be presented to us within those circumstances.

It needs to be remembered that we arise from pure energy and pure potentiality. Ultimately, we cannot help but become ours'elves. While others help us define ours'elves as we are attracted toward them or move away from them, this attraction, or lack thereof, always originates from our own s'elf. We are essentially and ultimately defined by our course through the Universe. We are Energy, with a particular Vibration and Frequency. That is our True Name and our True Nature. All we experience helps shape our being. But in the end, we are who we choose to be. And because we originate from pure potentiality, we can be anyone we choose, as long as we consistently put out our energy, which is to say we follow that choice with action. Action/magic is our primary mode of choice on this level of development. As we say, as we advance in our evolutionary development as Soulful Spirits, thoughts, actions, and magic will merge and our thoughts will be actions or acts of magic. However, for this to happen we need to attain full Mastery over our lower aspects of Spirit that manifest as robotic drives, urges and conflicting personality aspects.

Love is the primary power of the Soul. While our lower personalities often fear being overwhelmed by others, and there is good reason for this to be so, it need never fear the Soul, for the Soul never forces its way. It gives love freely and awaits in patience its eventual return.

The lower aspects of the Spirit naturally react to attempts to overwhelm it. It does so both because it is its nature at this point to secure the s'elf, but also because it has most likely experienced at some point, in this or a previous life, being tread upon by more potent Spirits that are themselves striving toward success and fulfillment in the world. This sense of s'elf that the Spirit promotes therefore helps protect the s'elf from incursions by predatory Spirits that are following the instinctual drive toward power without as yet having developed much in the way of Soulfulness. In fact, many of these sorts, particularly those of the Dark Lodge reject soulfulness altogether viewing the Soul as a weakness to be overcome.

These Dark Sorcerers, or perhaps more accurately we may call them Selfish Sorcerers, or even in some cases, Soul Diminished Sorcerers, tend to attract robotic level beings with underdeveloped Spirits. However, those beings who become their devoted followers are often soulfully developed in the lower stages. This in time creates a conflict in these followers who either must diminish their own souls, or in embracing their souls come into conflict with, or seek to escape from, the Dark Sorcerers. The Dark Sorcerers also make alliance with other Sorcerers of the same nature who unite with them for mutual benefit, but tend to surreptitiously vie with each other although not always, or perhaps seldom with the Master Sorcerer whom they know would crush them if they opposed hir. Master Sorcerers of this type, however, do vie intensely with other Master Sorcerers.

Elves, who tend to be advanced both in Spirit and in their higher Souls, often come into conflict, although not always intentionally, with these Charismatic Sorcerers and their followers/minions. We say not intentionally because we are often too wise to oppose them directly; however, neither can we acknowledge or participate in the fervor, madness and often violent prejudice that follows in their wake. However, these individuals are extremely paranoid, as previously indicated, and have the attitude that you are either with them or against them, and unless the elf shows fervent approval of them, they and their cohorts immediately will categorize hir as being evil. Understand that one doesn't have to directly oppose them to be seen as their enemy. Failure to cheer loudly enough may qualify one for that position. Sometimes to survive, we must pretend to be one of them, but our preferred method is always evasion and retreat until that time when we can take, or support, effective action in opposition to their deeds.

Thus it is also true that elves being born into modern societies often find ours'elves surrounded by less evolved spirits. We do not mean this to indicate that we are ultimately superior to them, for in the vast-vast, all are equal; but in the temporary circumstances of the world, we are frequently surrounded by those who are eager to be followers of the charismatic sorcerer types, some of whom alas, but not all, have greater Spirit development than Soul development. Those followers with greater Spirit development tend thus toward the sorcerer's path, the path that begins in its earliest stages with the practice of manipulating others. Therefore, we elves often feel alienated in our early lives, knowing ours'elves to be different than those around us, since we have far less inclination to be followers than they, and tend in time to develop a disinterest in manipulating others, which is to say we have no wish for followers. Rather, we seek union with equals and thus hunger ever for our own kind.

Our developed Spirit will not let us conform easily to those who are not in fact soulfully developed, yet our soulful natures still urges us toward union. This can be a difficult period for the newly awakened, or even unawakened Elfae for until we find at least one other of our kind with whom to relate and by this relationship anchor ours'elves, we frequently feel that we just don't belong in this world, with the consequential urge to escape elsewhere, in our fantasies, if in no other way.

However, this alienation also has a positive side, for in our alienation from the world our openness to Elfin becomes stronger as we reach out for what is True in Life and the Call of Faerie responds to us. This Call of Faerie is our Soul/Spirit calling to us from the realms of actualized potentiality. That is to say it is from the perfected s'elf we are destined to be as reflected in those who have already achieved this more perfected state of s'elfhood and to whom we are naturally and eternally connected. In other words, our evolved elfin kin, the Shining Ones, ever call to us and send us help and guidance.

Training the Dog

In a way, we could compare the disciplining or attaining mastery over the lower, or robotic aspects of the s'elf, to training a dog. Of course, different people have different ideas about training dogs, some are harsh and very strict, some are of an overly indulgent nature; however, most do love their dog and train it so that it can function in their home and in the world effectively. Naturally, the dog, like the lower self, wants to do what it wants to do, which is often run amuck in the world, but it is in the dog's best interest to be trained, particularly when done in a loving and compassionate way. It needs to know who is boss, or the leader of the pack, so to speak, but it also needs to know that it is valued for its place in the pack.

This is also the case of the lower self, which not being us, but forming a temporary alliance with us, also needs training and benefits from this training. These temporary aspects of our s'elf are also born of the Source, carry the Divine potentiality with their own s'elves, and will, in time, evolve into their own true beings and nature. They are literally here to gain training from us that will hold them in good stead in their own evolutionary path. Thoughts, as we said, are things; and all things are destined to evolve into their perfected natures.

Naturally, the lower aspects of the s'elf at first resist this training or discipline that we seek to impose upon it. It wants what it wants. However, again like training a dog, encouragement and rewards are an effective means of developing mastery over these lower aspects. Behavioral modification is very effective upon the lower order of beings, and aspects of being. The most important thing, however, in training a dog or the lower s'elf is the love one has for it. It is important to have the best interests of the lower self in one's heart when training it, and truly it is in the best interest of that self to be trained. Just as it is in our best interest as evolving beings to be educated/trained to develop to the fullest extent our abilities and skills, our intellect and personalities.

The Power of Reason

The power of reason masters the impulsive nature. Therefore, there are those who exult the mind and the intellect over the lower s'elf, which is primarily ruled by passionate drives and impulsive urges. This is an important stage, but, it is an intermediate stage of development; however, two things need to be remembered concerning this. First, reason, while an extremely valuable tool, is limited. Reason is important, but too often reason devolves into rationalization. And reasoning is only effective when one has accurate data upon which to reason. At the far reaches of reason is intuition, where one analyzes the data and reasons as best one can and then intuits or theorizes/hypothesizes beyond that, then one tests one's hypotheses against the data one has. This is essentially the scientific method, and it is valuable when used to rise above the lower nature, and yet it still needs to understand its own limitations. We must seek thus to be ever honest with and about our own s'elves, our strengths and weaknesses, our skills, abilities and our tendencies toward temptation.

Rationalizations usually arise from the introduction of false premises and data, false assumptions that often are an incursion of the lower self surreptitiously masquerading as reason or intellect. And while true reason is an invaluable tool for mastering the lower nature, it is still lacking when devoid of the influence of the Soul. The Soul's only reason is Love. The Spirit's reason is the success of the s'elf though the accumulation of knowledge = power. The Spirit trains the s'elf to reason. The Soul encourages its advancement out of love. The Spirit says watch me, Mommy, the Mother Soul watches, smiles, and says, "Wonderful."

Understanding the Student

The first thing every effective teacher does is to discover the interests, strengths, and abilities of those who come to one requesting to be taught or trained. One starts with where the student is and what sHe desires, and the ways sHe learns most easily and proceeds from there. So, too, in training our own lower selves, we may proceed most effectively by understanding what its desires are, and how these can be utilized to train it. So, also, in training our more developed s'elves, we need to follow our own interests and connect all that we learn, or need to learn to achieve our goals, to what we already know. The Path to Elfin and higher evolution is ever a s'elf chosen path for how are we to discover our True S'elves if we don't follow our true interests, whatever they may be at a particular moment?

Of course, life is seldom perfect. We are, after all, moving toward perfection. Often we are compelled to learn things that we have little interest in, thus we tend not to learn them, or to learn them poorly. However, all knowledge is valuable and as one rises in Spiritual/Spirit development, one also becomes one's own teacher, by which we mean, we actively integrate all information we encounter. We accept the hints of fate and karma, knowing that they are servants of our destiny, and we learn all we can about everything that comes to us. First, of course, we must learn to overcome our own resistance to learning, which is a hold over from the lower aspects of personality that want only what they want and which lack a more expansive vision that we obtain as we advanced in Spirit and Soulfulness. The Soul embraces all things; the Spirit turns all things to its own advantage.

In time, we come to realize that the inevitable becomes harder when we resist it. We can hate learning certain things, or doing certain things, and make ours'elves miserable in the process, or we can learn to love learning and doing, and mastering the techniques needed and the circumstances that confront us by doing so. Take, for instance, doing dishes, or housework in general. Most of us do not relish these tasks, and in resisting them we struggle both with them and our own s'elves. However, we when accept these tasks and decide to love doing them, they become easier, and enjoyable. Not only that, but as we advance as elven magicians, sorcerers, witches and wizards, we also learn how such rituals can be used to instill our lives and our environments with magic, and we transform a mundane task into a spell of power. And as we do this we become better at doing these chores and they become easier to do. In time, elven magicians turn every act into an act of magic, which is just an acknowledgement of what we come to realize is a fact of existence. All things originate from the Source, which is the Magic, and thus all things bear the potential of that magic within them.

On With the Dance of Romance

Every Spirit hungers for recognition or communion. For the Soulfully diminished Spirits this is a need for recognition from one's fans or followers, a validation of the importance of their self worth. For many advanced Spirits, that is the Soulfully developed, this recognition manifests itself as the influence of the Divine, of Elfin/Faerie manifest and reaching out to embrace the individual.

Alas, on the lower planes of being, this hunger, like all hungers, must be continually feed. The Dark Sorcerer seeks constant affirmation of hir potency and power. Often for these it functions in a dark, negative or opposite fashion. That is they feel empowered by harming or destroying others, rather than uniting with them. Psychologically, if you dig deep enough you will find these individuals fear powerlessness and rejection. However, even in rejecting the Soul, the Soul is acknowledged. The hunger remains and it will never be truly satisfied until it evolves to that higher state of positive, healing union.

So it is that television and movie stars sometimes commit suicide, even though it would seem on the outside that they have everything to live for. Often very rich and successful business people come to the end of their lives and still wonder what it was all about. This hunger, this Soulful yearning, this dissatisfaction with the world as it is, the sense that even with all one has accomplished there is still more, the never ceasing drive to eat, consume, shop, become intoxicated or fornicate, are all hungers, on various levels of development that reflect the Spirit's hunger for the Soulful. Though we may wander down many dark alleys and dead end streets in our search for Elfin, though we may give up at times and cry out in anguish, in all these ways we still acknowledge the search, the Quest, for what is True and Real. At some point, we come to the realization that we can only become ours'elves by going beyond ours'elves, by becoming more than we currently are.

But in saying that we don't mean, as so many seem to think, that we will dissolve into nothingness, as some suppose to be the case with death, and become a part of the whole but no longer exist as our s'elves. That is in reality the place where we began. It is not, however, where we are heading. The Soul wants us to be ours'elves. It does not wish to rid us of our Spirits but to development our Spirits to their fullest extent. The Soul loves us. It wants what we want only from a more mature, evolved and wiser perspective. It wants the best for us; it wants us to be our best. The nature of the Universe is not meant to be bland and uniform, but spectacular and harmonious. In the long run, only you can limit yours'elf by your own nature. And when that nature is in harmony with all things, all things become possible.

One of Silver, One of Gold

In Elven lore, as well as in the Bible, there are two trees in the Garden of Paradise or the Realm of the Divine: one of Silver, one of Gold. In the Bible, one tree bears the apple that grants the power of the Knowledge of Good and Evil, which we would call the Power of Reasoning, which helps us attain Mastery over the lower aspects of the s'elf and of the world, and the other tree is the Tree of Life Eternal. In Chinese lore, this second tree bears peaches whose nectar grants immortality. These trees represent the two drives of life, Success/Happiness/Pleasure and Immortality. The Spirit seeks both of these aspects, or powers of being; and the Soul seeks them as well although in a different fashion, as we've pointed out previously.

Both these trees grow at the heart of Faerie and are feed by the Sacred Spring that is life, the Source, the Divine Magic and they extend their branches throughout the worlds. The more we gain mastery over our s'elves, the closer we come to these trees, the more we are able to function in harmony with others, the greater our potentiality for gaining mastery over our own s'elves. The Spirit is the Artist, but the Soul is the Muse.

The roots of these trees dip down into the Source, and the branches reach out everywhere, extending through the dimensions or parallel worlds. As the Spirit climbs the trees, which are intertwined, it gains ever greater mastery over its'elf; and becomes, if it reaches the upper branches, ever more soulful. But what happens when it reaches the top, when the S'elf has indeed become its'elf? Then it reaches down and helps others to ascend. The more soulful we become, the more we aid our others to become their own s'elves. We do not need to sacrifice our Spirits, our S'elves to do this, as so many religious and spiritual groups tell us, but rather by being our perfected s'elves we vibrate as a living example that inspires others. We become Artist and Muse.

And in fact, the height of our art is the awakening of the spirit and soulfulness in others. The greatest art is the most inspiring. Yet, we do not create our art to inspire, but do it for its own sake, for love of the art. It is that love, that soulfulness that ultimately makes it inspiring. True Magic doesn't involve an attempt to do magic. Magic flows naturally from us with no effort at all except the effort to be the best we can be in every circumstance, and every moment.

And just as a good parent delights in and encourages the success of its child, so also the Soul ever delights in and always encourages the Spirit. And just as the two trees intertwine as they grow upward so do we become ever more Soulful as Spirits knowing increasingly that our success and progress, and the success and progress of our others, is intimately intertwined. If an elf arrives in Elfin and no one is there, sHe will immediately set forth again, after a refreshing sip from the Sacred Spring, to find hir others. Or sHe will begin singing the Star Songs that will guide them there.

Do you hear that, beloved? It is the Song of the Stars calling us home to Elfin being sung by our beloved kindred who await us.

Joining the Dance

Of course, one does not need to be in the center of Elfin to sing the Star Songs, although the acoustics there are amazing whose vibrates radiate outward throughout the Dimensions. Nor does one need to have fully come to be one's true s'elf as a Spirit to Soulfully reach out to one's kindred. In fact, as we've endeavored to indicate, each one leads to the other. The more we help our others the more soulful we become, and the more soulful we become the more we desire to help our others. At the same time, the more we become our true s'elves as evolved Spirits, the more we come to recognize and acknowledge that spirit in others. Without the Soulful influence, the Quest becomes a competition for recognition as demonstrated by the Soul Diminished or Soul Lacking. As we become Soulful, it becomes a mutually appreciative recognition that is inspiring to all concerned.

Giving the Devil his Due

While we may despise, fear, or even pity the Dark Sorcerers, think of Hitler, they as Spirits often have, in fact nearly always have, some quite amazing abilities and powers. And while we do not support or admire the deeds they commit in their Will to Power, we none-the-less cannot help but admire their mastery. It is ever unwise to underestimate those who have chosen to be one's enemy. And while they may do things that we view as being bad or evil, and create tremendous suffering and misery in the world for thousands, even millions of people, it is always wise to encourage the good in everyone, for the Divine exists in potential in all beings. The Divine is an essential part of every being's nature, even if that individual hasn't as yet realized, that is made it real, in hir own life.

The admonition to look for the good in everyone is not simply a nice saying; it is a soulful understanding, as well as a soulful urge, to foster in a positive way every individual. It is also a potent magic. Some individuals are not yet at a point where such positive encouragement, or encouragement of the positive really, has much effect upon them, but really that is more their problem than ours.

Seeing Beyond the World

We tend to see things from where we are at the moment with the added influence of the things we remember and have experienced previously. Thus in high school we often tend to think our high school activities and rivalries are very important. But as we move on to college or adult life we often realize how unimportant the issues of that time were. So, too, the world we live in and incarnate in over and over seems quite important to us, and it is every time, but as we develop as Spirits and Souls we tend to move beyond those realms of concern to more expansive realms and the concerns of this time seem not so very important anymore.

This greater understanding does not relieve us of doing our duty in the world, but as we evolve, the concerns that captured our attention and took up so much of our energy previously become mere memories quickly fading of things past, and unless we delve into the Akashic Record, we tend to forget them altogether as they become assigned to the great Unconscious. The more soulful we become the wider our reach, our experience and our understanding, and we begin to recognize these for the true powers that they are.

On the lower reaches one often confuses force for power, but elves know that true power does not attempt to force things, it enchants. It is not that force is never used, but that it is most powerful when least used and applied precisely. The greatest victory is attained when one wins without fighting. To the elven, the great powers are not psycho-kinesis and other mundane powers, although they are pretty cool, but Love, Courtesy, and Personality. While all elves pursue with vigor our own true natures and insist on pursuing our own path, few of us ever conceive of an Elfin without our others. Elfin in our minds and hearts is always the place of the great Reunion, where having shaped ours'elves through the worlds and dimensions we come again to gather and renew ours'elves and each other. Elfin in many ways is born of the marriage of Soul and Spirit.

The Great Spirit

What most individuals consider to be God or the Great Spirit is indeed an individuated being/power that has risen through the eons of evolutionary development and attained great influence and the powers to create/effect the world. Of course, different faiths have different ideas of this/these being/s, some more loving and kind, some more severe, some concerned for our well-being, some just plain disinterested. However, in as much as this Great Spirit is separate from its creation, it is a manifestation of a particularized Spirit. The degree of this being's relationship to, and interaction with, those beings that compose its creation, indicates the degree of Soulful development of this great power. Such beings are essentially demi-gods and each of us is destined to be the god-dess of our own universe of magic in the course of time.

The Great Soul

To the elves, the Divine is inherent in the nature of the Universe. It lives in potential in all things/beings and is to be realized there. This would be the Great Soul, the underlying unity and unifying element of Creation, the potential for perfection and harmony. Scientifically we might consider this Gravity, that mysterious power that draws us together. However, more poetically we may call it Love. Those who say that God is Love are correct from an Elven point of view.

If we consider Soul to be gravity, we might view Spirit as the movement toward expansion in the Universe. At the same time, we may view Spirit and Soul as electromagnetism. Spirit creates electric charge and then creates magnetism or Soul. In simple terms, we might say we are attracted to interesting, Spirit evolved individuals, or individuals who are filled with Spirit. Great Spirits are incredibly attractive. There is nothing sexier and more fascinating than an individual filled with Spirit.

More Old Elven Sayings:

> Few people take the elfin very seriously, which is just as well for when they do so they tend to terrify thems'elves unnecessarily.

> Cleverness is greatly appreciated by we elfin but not valued nearly as much as kindness and sincerity.

> It is easier and, in the long run, quicker to do things correctly the first time, although not always as educational

> We have said that organizing elves is like herding cats, but among ours'elves we say that organizing elfin is like reasoning with a fanatic. You can try to do it, but it is unlikely to have any effect and is generally a waste of time.

> Organizing elves is a bit like herding cats, only elves are less likely to scratch you and cats are less likely to take you by the hand and start dancing around you singing a song.

> Every elf awakens in hir own time. And what is hir own time?
> It is not merely the time when the elf is ready
> but the time that was destined since time immemorial,
> hiding within the elf's own psyche and triggered
> by events whose very nature leads one to believe
> and know that their Destiny and Elfin have spoken.

> Those who argue with elves usually find themselves
> caught in a trap of their own devising.

> Elves almost never raise their voices except in song and celebration.

> If we elves have failed to live up to your expectations,
> we apologize. However, it is quite enough for us to endeavor
> to live up to our own expectations for ours'elves each day.

> If you wish to know the truth of elves, listen to our dreams.
> In our visions everything is revealed. Our imaginations shape reality.

Section Two:

The Elven Way

> *We are told that eventually nearly all magicians must choose between the left hand path or the right hand path. However, we elfin nearly always choose the two handed path.*
> —*The Silver Elves*

THE AWAKENING OF THE HIGHER INSTINCTS

As we've indicated, the lower urges and passions are mastered by the power of reason as well as the acts of magic we evoke through our behavior to foster or eliminate inferior aspects of being, including the demons of enculturated programming instilled in us at a very early age. But reason alone will only get us so far and every elf ultimately relies on hir instincts, particularly in situations where there are not enough facts or information to base logical decisions upon. When the lower drives and urges have been mastered, these instincts become a clear and reliable basis for our decisions. They come from our inner s'elves and our true natures; however, by its own very nature instinct evokes the Soul since it is a function of our being that reaches out beyond the s'elf. It is our sixth sense.

This evocation of the higher instincts in arousing the Soulful nature also evokes the intuitive faculty. It is a more direct, certain and a simpler mode of directive being. It knows instinctively, which is to say with inner surety, and as we come to trust it, it becomes a faithful guide for us. Most often in common parlance, this mode of instinctual guidance is referred to as following one's heart.

At first, however, the mind wishes to analyze these instinctual offerings, applying the elements of logic and reasoning to them. There is no great harm in this if one allows the higher instincts to guide one and uses the analytical faculty to observe and note the success and value of following its guidance. For these elves, and perhaps for most Elfae, failure to pay heed to this higher instinct has inevitably landed us in hot water, and led to innumerable difficulties that could have otherwise been avoided.

It should be noted that this higher instinct can not be controlled by the mind; it can only be allowed to function. The mind does not make it happen, it can only get out of the way so it can occur. Being an aspect of the evolved Soul, this higher instinct also can not urge us to do wrong to ours'elves or others, as may be the case at times with the lower instincts. In this way, it also functions as what is commonly called our conscience. It is this higher instinct that opens the way to the supernal realms and dimensions where the Shining Ones, our Elfae ancestors abide, and from which they guide our own evolution by means of hints and suggestions. The Soul being a unitive power is also therefore expansive, which is to say it continually adds to our being by increasing our contact and the ease of contact with other beings. The advanced Soul sees the world, the Universe, from a higher, wider, more inclusive view. In regards to all it does, it considers all to whom it is connected.

As the Soul is expansive in bringing things together and thus widening one's reach, the Spirit, in a sense, is contractive, it is ever defining, like a sculptor cutting away wood or stone to reveal/create an image beneath. We know that this is the opposite of what we said in terms of the expansive and attractive/gravitational nature for the Spirit/Soul just a few paragraphs previously, however, the Nature of Life is paradoxical and what we offer here are hints and suggestions, not absolutes. The Absolute Truth is within us. We cannot give it to you; you must discover it for your own s'elf. However, we may say the Soul expands us by linking us to others; the Spirit expands us as we become greater through this association. The Soul contracts in that it draws us together; the Spirit contracts in that it ever defines our uniqueness. This is reflected by the fact that there are those who see the people of the world becoming more and more in contact with each other, with wider and faster range of travel, often saying *the world is growing smaller*, even though one's range and possibilities are in fact ever increasing.

Old Souls and Old Spirits

In spiritual circles, people often speak of Old Souls. They are most often referring to very mature and wise beings who have clearly been on the evolutionary path of development for eons and eons. Of course, there are also ever those who refer to their own s'elves as being Old Souls and this, usually, is more of a proclamation of aspiration than one of reality. But the Old Souls, being the wise Souls that they are, and ever inclusive, do not deter these eagerly aspiring Spirits from their soulful calling. The Old Souls simply smile and nod and encourage them on their way.

Few, however, speak of Old Spirits, but the elven know that there are not only Old Souls, but Old Spirits as well. Old Spirits are very developed personalities. They are very unique, many would call them eccentric, beings who stand out from the mass of humanity. One knows there is something different about them, something special about them, but most are unsure exactly what that difference is.

Most Elfae are both Old Souls and Old Spirits, but we are still on the evolutionary path, and we are still following the Elven Way. While we are often more advanced in many ways than the mass of humanity, we also know that the difference between us is, when seen from the more subtle dimensions, quite small; otherwise we would most likely be elsewhere and not here. And we are also aware that even those who seem less advanced than we frequently have talents and abilities that we do not have.

The Soulfully aware know there is always something that can be learned from each and everyone, no matter what hir level of development; and that the Spark of the Divine burns in every Soul just awaiting the breath of another Soul to fan it into a flame. While we Elfae have been often, and for ages, ostracized by many of the social and ethnic groupings of humanity, who ever vie for dominance, we have come to realize that the means to mastering such beings is not by withdrawal, although sometimes we must do so for our safety, nor by attempting to dominate them in turn, but by embracing them from a higher state of realization. Thus we never accept their rejection of us, nor react to it. We ever follow our higher instincts, and pursue our own direction. We encourage their Soulfulness and their true Spirits; frequently we even admire them. But we have no obligation to be involved with these save as circumstance and fate demand. We accept them in their Divine Potential, but we do not necessarily involve ours'elves in their lives. Neither do we automatically reject them, our actions/our magic are ever based on our own sense of direction and intent. In this way, we become the Masters of our own Destiny.

How do we love them from a higher realm of being? By ever offering them courtesy and respect for their Spirits and their Souls. With courtesy the Elfae can attract such individuals, or send them on their way. With respect we encourage the development of their Souls and Spirits. Courtesy and respect are the basic policies, and the foremost magical powers, that all elves learn to use in interacting with others.

Trails and Tribulations

Over and over, one hears various spiritual and religious devotees tell us that God never gives us problems or troubles that we can't overcome. This is true in the long run of things, but in our temporary manifestations we find our bodies and our psyches facing overwhelming circumstances that lead to death or depression and a fractured mind, Soul, and Spirit. It happens, women are raped, children molested, innocents murdered, whole populations starve, millions live in poverty. How can that not be overwhelming at times?

Some will say that being raped or molested is the individual's karma, and this is true if you mean karma in terms of fate, that is the individual was born in an era when rape and molest still occur. We are not the cause of everything that befalls us, but we must accept responsibility for our actions and reactions if we are to advance to the higher/more subtle dimensions of being. That is the only way to gain power as magicians, sorcerers, and adepts, et al. Not everything that happens to an individual is a result of ill deeds they've committed in the past; sometimes we are knocked down by some Dark Sorcerer's selfish magic. Ours is not the only magic in the world, and it may happen that we are overpowered by someone else's spells.

However, sometimes we have simply taken on too much as a Spirit. When we are between bodies, and at the place where we choose or are drawn to our next incarnation, we sometimes in our passion to evolve, undertake paths that prove too great for us to master in the life we choose. We remember our mother saying to us when we were quite young and we'd fill our plate with food: that our eyes were bigger than our stomach. This is also the case with eager Spirits. Just as a student passionate to get through college and on to hir career will at times take on more courses than she can handle, or like a musician eager to learn the guitar so sHe practices until her fingers bleed, Spirit sometimes choose challenges that prove to be too great for them or which evokes tremendous suffering to quicken the process. This, however, is the tendency for younger Spirits, for what we may call teenage Spirits, and as one evolves one also realizes that slow and sure is often a quicker means to the goal than too much, too soon, too quick.

As the Spirit evolves, which is to say grows stronger, it can handle greater and greater obstacles. The evolved Spirit also attains a wider view and understanding of life. The awakened consciousness knows that the world as it appears to us is an illusion, a play of sorts, and knows that death is temporary. The Spirit develops fearlessness. Its goal becomes nearly everything to it, and it will face death itself with no compunction to achieve its ends. This fearlessness opens the Spirit to the Soul, for as it loses fear the individual Spirit finds it much easier to interact with others of all sorts. As it increasingly gains confidence in the indissolubility of its immortal nature the developing fearlessness encourages the individual to interact with other spirits more freely. This does not mean it acts unwisely, or carelessly with its life, but it gives the spirit a boldness that pervades its aura and all its actions.

It is true there are those who believe the world will always be filled with rape, molest, war and violence of various sorts, but these Spirits have limited vision and it will be many lifetimes before they can, or perhaps will bother, to look into the Vast. These immature Souls project the attitude that they know it all now. They tend to be absolute in their certainty; however, most often their view of a perpetually violent and cruel world is born of their own inability to release their personal fears or habits of being, such as meat eating that help perpetuate violence in the world. We do not blame these for their ignorance. They are where they are at this time; they know no more than they know. How can they? We do not choose our students; they choose us. We can only do our best to help each and everyone that comes to us and is genuinely ready to learn. Besides, we live in the backwater world just as they do, and are ever aware of this; yet, we see beyond.

So, beloved Elfae Spirits, as the old saying goes, try not to bite off more than you can chew. But if you do, know that you will rise from the dead, re-incarnate and try it all again. In many ways, evolution is like a video game, if you get killed; you can try again and again until you master each level. Life can be very difficult at times but as we develop as Spirits we come to understand that with persistence and perseverance we will master every difficulty, gaining skills and power as we do so. This is a difficult understanding to attain, particularly when we are in the midst of the game/life and filled with the passion and intensity of playing it; but it is one that will serve us well as we progress as spirits.

The Magician and the Mystic

The Way of the Spirit is the way of the Magician. The Magician/Spirit seeks to gain control over hir own s'elf and through that the ability to influence and manifest what sHe wants/desires/wills in the world.

The Mystic seeks communion with the Divine. It is, as we've said, a Soulful endeavor and frequently involves the overwhelming of the individual by the invocation of the Divine within the individual Spirit. These individuals open thems'elves to being a vehicle for the Divine. This can be seen, perhaps most clearly, in the Voudoun tradition where the practitioner becomes the *horse* for the particular god invoked. So, also, do individuals seek to have Jesus fill their Souls and act through them.

Paradoxically in many cases, Mystics are isolated individuals. They, like monks, separate themselves from the mass of humankind so there will be no distractions in their quest to unite with the Divine. But Mystics, and Monks, also frequently seek a life of service to the Divine, or for the Divine by which we mean the Mystics seeks to act on the behalf of the Divine in the world.

We elves perhaps can see this most clearly in our devotion to Santa Claus that great and wondrous Spirit. Each Yule we act on the behalf of this great Elf Spirit by giving presents in his name. We act in his stead and he manifests in the world through our actions. We are Santa's helpers; we are the elves that assist him. Yet, unlike the Mystics who often let the Spirit overwhelm them, we elves retain our individual Spirit even while acting in service to that Greater Spirit. So it is that we act in cooperation with the Shining Ones, those great elven spirits who are our ancestors, and who have advanced to the more subtle dimensions of Soulful Spirit. We manifest their spirit in the world though our own elven lives.

Leaders and Followers

We elves have been known to say that we have no leaders, nor followers. This is true in a strict sense, although in another sense we elves tend to be both leaders and followers. Our leaders are those who inspire us. Like all Spirits we seek Greater Spirits from whom to learn and to guide us on our way. Like all Souls, we seek to serve the Divine, as manifested through Great Spirits, to make the world a better place for all, as well as grow closer to the heart of Elfin.

However, we are never mindless followers who obey without questioning. Questioning, an essential part of the Quest, is also a vital part of the Elfae Spirit. We voluntarily assist those beings who we recognize as being pioneers upon the Path and who are experienced Spirits in the Elven Way. Our minds often analyze this path, but it is our higher instincts that tell us whether a particular byway upon the path is the right one for us.

As leaders, we are never strict authorities. It's simply not in our elfin nature to be so. The advanced nature of our Spirit and Soul lead us to reflect the higher aspects of the Spirit Souls above us, those great beings we call the Shining Ones, by guiding those who come to us with hints and suggestions. We do not demand. We do not set strict rules. We reveal the Way from our Vision, and see who decides for their own s'elves to follow it, assisting them to the best of our ability. But mostly, the Elven leader leads. The Elfae leader doesn't control others, sHe ventures ever on and if others wish to follow the path forged by hir progress, to expand it or pave it or diverge from it, that is up to them. Elven leaders are not authorities but visionaries and pioneers.

Elvenhome

Most elves, however, feel the call to community. These bright spirits create an Eald, a mini realm of Elfin/Faerie, where the Elfae may gather and pursue each hir own path, which usually means the pursuit of hir own art and creations. This comingling of elf spirits is usually achieved in a very loosely structured fashion. There is seldom more structure than is needed beyond the bare essentials to make the union work. Still, there is often an Elfae or two who are at the center of the union. These Soulfully developed Spirits attract elves to them by their advanced natures and the fearlessness with which they embrace those who come. These are powerful beings and developed Spirits. Particularly among elves, there are often several Elfae acting in concert who function as such a center of such a community, usually one or more powerfully advanced Spirits, and two or more Elfae who are Soulfully advanced. The great Spirits attract aspiring Elfae by the power of their personalities, and those great Souls nurture all who come. However, it should be noted that it seldom works if those involved have greater Spirit development than Soul development. Each advanced Spirit needs at least one or more Soulfully advanced Elfae to balance hir.

It is from such as these that the vibration of Elfin/Faerie, and those powers and secrets that can only be transmitted directly from one person/spirit/soul to another, are passed on. So when it is said that Elfae have neither leaders or followers, this is true; but we do have those who inspire us, guide us and set an example of advanced Elven Spirit and Soulfulness. And we also have those who assist them, and by doing so mystically serve the Spirit of Elfin/Faerie, as well as serving all those who come for guidance. As in the most ancient traditions, which is to say Elder/Eldar Traditions, the leader serves the people, the people serve the realm, and the realm, which is the land, protects and nurtures us all. The two trees are intertwined, spiraling around each other as they extend into the supra-dimensional realms of Elfin. Welcome to Elfin.

Elfland

You will notice we call it Elfin, or Faerie or Elfin/Faerie instead of Elfland as it is usually called in faery tales. This is because Elfin/Faerie is not a particular place on Earth or Elsewhere, but like the Divine lives in potential within all things, particularly within our own beings. Any elf, or any group of Elfae, by living their lives as elves and by establishing an Eald invites and awakens Elfin/Faerie to manifest within and through hir/them, and the vibrational region these individuals inhabit. Just as you can create a home in a place that you buy or rent so, too, does Elfin manifest wherever elves live. For Elfin is ever, and always, Elvenhome (Eldataelum ... pronounced L – day – tah – e – loom... : see our book *Arvyndase [SilverSpeech]: a short course in the language of the Silver Elves*). Wherever elves manifest, so does Elfin. Like Merlin's apple orchard that followed him wherever he went, so does Elfin appear wherever elves manifest, which is to say, wherever we live our lives as elves.

There are those who would like to establish Elfland on this planet in the same way that there is France or Japan, to have Elfland be another country among the many existing countries. We have no difficulty with that aspiration, however, these elves (the authors) are, as are most elves, aspiring toward the supra-dimensions. We are not seeking to create an Elfland that is another country among many others, but to awaken Elfin upon the Earth, among the stars, and throughout the dimensions wherever we may wander. We are Gypsy Elves, and Elfin goes wherever we go.

It is said that home is where the heart/Soul is, which means Elvenhome is where elves gather. When one or more elves manifest as Elfin Spirits, the spirit of the Elfae, Elfin awakens. It is in many ways, the soulful interconnection of the elven that creates Faerie. We might ask then, if there were no elves manifest, would there be an Elfin/Faerie? And the answer is yes. It would still live in potential as all things do. However, it is by our lives, by manifesting our elven natures, that we make it real; and it is by our shared love, auras and connections that we weave it in the world. Welcome to Elfin, beloved, welcome home.

Serenity

This call to Elvenhome and Elven Community or Elven Frasority (combining the words fraternity and sorority and indicates an equal union of female and male, which is the way of the elves) that is felt so strongly by most Elfae is the Call of Elfin/Faerie. It manifests in our Souls as a hunger for union and as such it invites us, intrigues us, and enchants us to change and develop in order to come closer and closer to its realization. But in time it also manifests as a realization. It awakens within us, not as a hunger, but like a soothing breeze that whispers magic to our Soul and heals us and fills us with a sense of serenity.

One of the techniques, as we mentioned earlier in this tome, to quieting the mind and gaining Mastery over the lower aspects of the s'elf is meditation, used by elves and others in two basic forms, observing the mind chatter without feeding it, and thus letting it starve and eventually cease, and spell or mantra meditation, focusing on a particular word of power or spell and influencing the world and one's s'elf thereby, while at the same time developing mental focus and power.

However, having done this successfully, the Soul begins to awaken and its response includes this feeling of Elvenhome that at times floods one's body, fills one with a soothing ecstatic sense, and a realization that one has at last come home and is with those with whom one is meant to be. It also bears with it an inner certainty that despite any indications to the contrary the evolution of our species is proceeding as planned.

This feeling of Eldataelum, of Elvenhome, which often comes to us and feels like it is a memory from our childhood, of ancient times, of future possibilities, and the sense of magic we had as children, is another meditation for the Elfae, a deeper meditation born of feeling rather than mental chatter. This sense of being at home at last, this sense of childhood magic, is a communion with our Soul, and by holding this feeling gently within us we begin to vibrate that energy out into the world.

Like the earlier form of meditation, it can be inconsistent at first. The feeling comes and goes as it will and we can but focus on it, sense it really, hold it gently and delicately within us as we would hold a fragile bird, and carry it with us as long as we can. Usually the concerns of the world, the circumstances of our life banish it soon enough, but having felt it a few times we begin to get a greater sense of it and in time we can summon it at will. We become the energy of Elvenhome; we are the Living Vibration of the Voice of Elfin calling to other elves in the world.

This can seldom happen, however, until one's Spirit is strong enough to cease seeking to define and empower its'elf at every moment. In this meditation, we become the child-like beings that Sages through the ages have told us reflects the nature of Wisdom. We are open, eager, ready to learn and filled with energy; at the same time we are satisfied, happy and content. We are again the ancient child-like elfin, old and young at the same time.

It is important to understand that this meditation consists not of a thought, although we must describe it here using thoughts, but a pure feeling. We feel fulfilled within ours'elves and connected to Elfin at the same time. This is a merging of the Spirit and the Soulful nature. We are ours'elves and we are in harmony with our others. This is a feeling of love, but not simply in a romantic way, although it does not preclude romantic feelings, but is more expansive and inclusive and more child-like. There is no fear of losing the S'elf, the unique individual Spirit; in fact it is clear that such an event isn't even possible.

As this feeling expands, it encompasses not only one's immediate environment but connects one with Elfae everywhere, and eventually with the Cosmos as a whole. We become one with Life, one with Elfin/Faerie, one with the Source from which the Divine Magic arises, and being so connected we partake of its Magic and its Powers.

Needless to say, when one is experiencing this meditative feeling of Elvenhome, all fears, worries and anxieties vanish. The opposite is also true, when one is experiencing fears, worries and anxieties one doesn't feel this sense of Elvenhome. However, the adept Elfae can take steps to first calm the mind with primary meditation, and then invoke this sense of Elvenhome, of being connected deeply and intimately with Elfin/Faerie, and thus with all one's kindred throughout the dimensions, and in this way summon this feeling.

The more one is able to invoke this feeling, the less anxieties one experiences. Since worries and anxieties cause stress, which is so very unhealthy, this meditation is productive of healing. Also, the less stress one feels in encountering the world, the less and less difficult it is to deal with any obstructions that arise. Life becomes easier for the most part as one masters this feeling connection to Elfin. One feels as if one's life is graced, which it is. The more one can invoke this feeling sense, the easier it becomes to do so. Like with nearly all things, determined and consistent practice makes perfect, which is to say brings mastery.

And as one develops this ability, this power to invoke this feeling, and therefore feels ever closer to Elfin/Faerie, the greater one's Vision becomes. One sees beyond the petty concerns of day-to-day life, which doesn't mean one doesn't still have to deal with them, but dealing with them becomes more and more easy. The trials and tribulations of this current incarnation are no more than another set of dishes to wash, a task that requires doing, but in and of itself is not significant except in as much as we turn it into an act of magic. We give it meaning through our magic. We master our lives by mastering the circumstances of our lives, which are the lessons of this incarnation, and turn our every act, and thus our Life, into an act of magic.

And as we invoke this sense of Elvenhome, and thus connect with our kindred throughout the dimensions, we also open ours'elves to the hints and suggestions that the Shining Ones send forth to help their kindred everywhere. The Shining Ones, who guide us ever, communicate with us by this means, and we will find our way to Elfin as surely as a lost dog can find his way home even if he is left thousands of miles away using his homing instinct. This feeling is our homing instinct. However, Elfin/Faerie is not out there somewhere for us to find, so much as within us to be awakened. What we are homing upon is not a place, but our inner sense of connection to Elfin, and to our beloved kindred. This feeling draws us together and by our sense of union Elfin comes into being wherever we may be.

This is because this feeling of Elvenhome is a soulful development of those higher instincts that we aroused as we began evoking our Soulful natures. It does not replace these instincts, which still function when needed for personal directional guidance and decision-making, but it adds to them. Those instincts in themselves give us a feeling of certainty, but they don't necessarily give us the sense of peace and at-home-ness that comes as they expand and develop. The instincts are a function of the Spirit, but they evoke the Soul, and as we become more soulful, that is ever more connected to Elfin, these instincts become ever more profound in their manifestation.

In fact, that is one aspect of their development, a sense of profundity that fills our being and assures us that Life, our life, is indeed meaningful and that there is purpose to Life overall, and a purpose to our individual life. Thus, this sense not only promotes physical health, but even more so it promotes the health of the psyche, for these are intimately intertwined.

One might think that in the invocation or the arousal of this feeling of Elvenhome, one might be inclined toward a desperate feeling of loss, of looking about and despairing that Elfin is not here. But the opposite is true. This feeling sense of Elvenhome is not one of Elfin being out there somewhere distant and separate from us, but that it is here now within us, and we are ever connected to it, cannot be separated from it, and will always find our kindred through the dimensions. It is a feeling of intimacy, of oneness and connectedness. It does not provoke despair, but quite the opposite. It awakens our faith and certainty of the Magic, the Source of All Being.

And when it passes, in those moments when it proves fleeting and moves on, it leaves us with a lingering sense of its passing. Like a kiss that we still feel after it has finished, it gifts us with a promise of more to come. We might despair that it has passed, or worry that it will not come again, but we need to remember that despair and worry prevent its arrival or invocation, and when we realize this, and apply ours'elves again to the meditative magics that invoke this sense/feeling in the first place, we do so with the certainty that our kindred are reaching out to us just as we are reaching out to them. Just as we now are calling out to you, beloved kin, can you feel it?

Hope Springs Eternal

From the center of Elfin/Faerie, in the heart of the Magic, issues the Sacred Spring of Life Eternal and Happiness Everlasting. From this Spring, the Blessed Trees grow spreading their branches through the dimensions. Every elf carries at least a drop of water from this Spring within hir Soul. And like water everywhere, each drop is complete on its own, and each unites easily with its others. If you strike it with a sword it is unharmed, as elves unseen among the trees. If you burn it with fire, it transforms and retreats into evaporation turning into the Mists of Faerie. If fierce winds blow it, it dances becoming the Faerie Circle. If earth absorbs it, it is still there, the Elfin Magic within.

From this Spring, hope arises awakening the Powers of the Wisdom that is Love. The human body is at least 60% water. While the waters of the Sacred Spring are not material in nature, none-the-less, they call to all water, they speak through all water, thus we can always hear the Call of Elfin by heeding our own true feelings that echo from the waters within. That Soulful drop from the Sacred Spring is transformative in nature, as we heed the Call of Elfin, awaken that vibration within us, it gradually transforms the mundane waters of our bodies into the sacred water from that Spring.

As we pointed out in our *The Book of Elven Magick, volume 2*, this Sacred Spring is, esoterically speaking, also the Mirror of Galadriel; it is a magic mirror into which one can look to see the Source that encompasses the realms of possibility: what is, what was, and what may or may not come to be … all that is possible. It is also the link to the Akashic Record, all that was and the interconnections, the probability threads, as they weave toward the future.

Thus, from this Spring flows knowledge, and while this knowledge can be sorted and analyzed in numerous way, as mathematical understanding, scientific exploration, psychological comprehension and any other form of knowledge, it is all still from one Source, and everything is related to everything else. For this is the secret of the Soul, every drop complete on its own, every drop connected to the whole, all are One together.

All religions, all spiritual philosophies, including this one, all racial groups, all ethnic groups, all stem from this source and all are connected, and though we may use different terminologies to describe how we view the world and the paths for navigating it, it is still one vast Ocean of Light, Life and Consciousness.

By understanding our connection to the All of Life and to all within it, we move from being trapped into a particular incarnation to sensing, seeing and understanding our immortal beings that span the lifetimes and are related to All that is. It is not important that we are called Elves, but that we are elves in our being, which is to say we understand our magical natures, and the potential magic in all others, and we live our lives with that awareness. This makes us elves in reality, whatever we or anyone may call us.

Why Do We Call Ours'elves Elves

One might wonder, if all is One and we are One with All, why do we bother to call ours'elves elves? Or anything at all, for that matter?

We could, of course, not call ours'elves anything. We could reject any identity at all in a mystical attempt to be ever united with the Absolute Undifferentiated Potentiality that is the underlying reality of all energy. We could thus seek to dissolve ours'elves back into the Void that Is, but really we'd still become our own S'elves. In a sense, to reject one's identity is like walking around naked all the time, which is okay with us if someone wants to do that, however, no bodies are the same and even if one eschews clothes in an attempt to be like everyone else, one is still ones'elf. Even if we all wear the same clothes, as certain societies would have us do to promote unity or conformity, we'd still be ours'elves.

The word Elves, of course, is just a name, a bit of nomenclature. We could call ours'elves, Flower Children, which we have, Star Children, that too, Space Gypsies, also that, and many other things that we have an inner sense of relating to. These elves don't call ours'elves dwarves because that title and the characters and aspects related to it, do not appeal to us, but obviously it does to others. We associate ours'elves with those things that attract us, and we are ever attracted to our own s'elves. Thus, as Spirits as we choose or create a culture to which to relate, we define ours'elves, we create or sub-create, co-create our own worlds, which is what we are here to do. However, as Souls we ever remember that we are connected to all other Spirits, and that a mutual respect for each other leads us to that place of harmony where we can each be ours'elves together (a thought form of the dawning Aquarian Age). We are all from the same source, but we are not all the same. The directions toward which we have spread out from the Center/Source defines us. We are each heading on our own Way. Some of us, however, are very close to each other as we do so, more or less headed in the same or similar direction.

But we feel it is important to consider that if we create our world in such a complicated and rule bound fashion, as some religions do, that the individuals following the way lose the ability to contact the Source through the direct communication of their own Souls, which happens when we lose compassion and respect for others, then we have certainly lost our Way. Thus we elves say that an Elfin composed only of Elves wouldn't be Elven at all.

Finding the Source

So how do we find our way back to the Source once we have developed our Spirits? We don't. Instead, we find the Source within us. By awakening the sense of Elvenhome, by awakening our Souls, we arouse that drop of the Sacred Spring that each of us carries, we radiate it from our beings, our lives, and we become the Source. The Sacred Spring is not in one place, but many. It lives in the being of every awakened Elfae, every sincere and genuine aspirant upon the path of enlightenment.

Naturally, each place, each being alive with the Power of the Sacred Spring, calls out to others who are so awakened, as well as arousing the drop of Magic in everyone sHe encounters, although many do not quite understand that feeling that is stirring in them or even who set it humming. But for the awakened, we recognize each other intuitively, a sense of déjà vu occurs. Do we know each other from another lifetime, or are we just remembering being in the Source together, the womb of all Life? Are we all meant to be together? Yes. But not all in the same place at the same time. If we follow our natural attractions and inclinations, we will find the right way for us, and the right companions.

How Do We Know What Is True?

Really, we need to ask ours'elves, how do we know what is true for us? First, we must trust ours'elves, our instincts, intuitions and our natural attractions. If we are true to ours'elves, without going out of our way to obstruct others, we will find the right way for ours'elves. In its essence, it is just that simple.

Second, for those things immediately beyond our understanding, such as what happens when we die, etc., what is the meaning of life, and other such questions that science as yet doesn't have definitive answers to offer us, we need to apply our reason, logic and an observation of the world based on the axioms As Above/So Below and As Within/So Within, and vice versa, by which we mean the reflection goes both way. The

Universe is a connected whole. Every part is linked esoterically to every other part, and to understand ours'elves we need to look beyond ours'elves, and to understand the Vast we need to look within our s'elves.

The main thing is, the most important thing to each of us now is, where do we go from here? And again, that you can only know by coming to trust yours'elf and your own sense of direction, by trusting your natural attractions. There is a reason you are attracted to certain things and not others; there is a reason you are interested in some things more than others; and there is a reason these interests change, develop and grow. And if you find yours'elf at a place were you absolutely don't know what to do or where to go: then wait and be patient, further directions will come in time. And if you find you are too impatient to wait, then search haphazardly. Let whimsy guide you.

And remember, dear Kindred, we are Calling to you. Even if we are no longer incarnate in these particular bodies when you read this, even if we are no longer in the same dimension, if you open yours'elf to your Elfin nature, you will hear the Call, awake a sense of Elvenhome within, and be guided surely to your own beloved kindred.

You Are Your Own Master

It is true that we learn from others, and it is also true there are certain energetic vibrations that can only be passed from one person to another. But, even alone the Spirit is a microcosm of the macrocosm (As Above/So Below) and all that is in the Universe can be found in essence within us. However, the Path is much more easily tread when we have good company to assist us.

We do not, however, need perpetual masters. We are each destined to attain Mastery of our own s'elves, to be our own Masters and while there are those, particularly the young and inexperienced Spirits who declare that mastery long before they are even close to achieving it, still the fact remains: you are destined to be the Master of your own s'elf.

And while we may make discoveries along the way, develop our abilities and our powers, hone our techniques and polish our personalities, all we need to know is ever and always available to us. It is always we who must make the effort and develop the skills in order to open ours'elves to it. As the saying goes, there is nothing new under the sun, or among the stars, save that we make it so by creating new and interesting combinations. All that is, was, or will be exists in potentiality in the Ever Present Now.

However, one must be a very developed Spirit, indeed, to proceed on one's own unaided, and most of us elves prefer the company of our others. This companionship is also very satisfying to our Soulful nature, and in acting together our powers increase exponentially. Alas, it is just at the very beginning of treading the Path of the Elven Way that one must often do so alone, at that very time when it would seem that the elf is least developed as a Spirit. Yet, the fact is that one must have achieved a certain level of Spirit development to dare to call ones'elf an elf at all in this world. And while there may be times when one wonders if there are any other Elfae anywhere near them, or if one will ever find one's others, it is this isolation that, while difficult, leads one to concentrate on the Song of the Stars, the Call of Elfin within one. And it is this effort to focus on the Call of Elfin that will in fact draw one's others to hir, and make hir stronger as a Spirit and more Soulfully aware.

These periods of aloneness, are often a test for the Elfae, they help us discover how genuine is our aspiration, how determined our devotion to the path, and how powerful our Spirit has become. If we use these periods to hone our Spirit and polish our personality, we become ever greater as Elfin Spirits, and the more powerful and developed we are as a Spirit, the more easily we attract our others. The never-ending effort to perfect the S'elf is the key to all we desire.

The Thousandth Elfae

You've heard of the 100th monkey theory surely. A monkey develops a new and improve technique for doing something, another monkey sees it and imitates it, others learn as well, and when the 100th monkey learns it suddenly, magically, all monkeys know it. It has entered the collective unconscious of monkey kind. The same is true of elves. After an elf awakens, if hir Spirit is strong enough to persevere, for it is at the very early stages when the elf strives on alone that so many fade from Elfin, sHe will in time attract others to hir. When there are two or more elves together, other Elfae will begin manifesting here and there as well; when there are a hundred, we begin to spread about the globe; when the thousandth Elfae awakens it begins a worldwide phenomena and Elfae everywhere sense a stirring in their Souls, the Call of Elfin grows every stronger, and our culture flourishes as the threshold within is reflected beyond. Elfin truly begins to manifest in the world.

Facts and Knowledge

Most of what people know, or think they know, are merely opinions, which can vary greatly according to the individual and hir current level of development. Even those things that we can take as demonstrated scientific fact are not always the same everywhere. The principles of Newtonian physics do not necessarily apply out among the Stars. Thus there is knowledge that is valid in some places but not in others. At the Source, where knowledge is Absolute, it is also less limited. While we are greatly bound by the limitations of the world or dimension we inhabit, the closer we get to Elfin/Faerie the greater our abilities to do magic, or perform what on this plane of existence would seem to be miracles. Thus Thaumaturges (miracle workers) are most often those who are advanced Spirits and are close to and in touch with the Source.

Greater knowledge, a more advanced understanding, always trumps and transcends lesser knowledge giving us greater power and abilities to function in whatever world we inhabit. The child in the first grade may have a very difficult time imagining what it is like to be in graduate school, but the graduate student can understand through experience and memory the challenges of first grade, although, even so the graduate student may not be eager to face them again. In fact, for most elves, one of the things that most disturbs us about dying is the thought that we will have to suffer through potty training and elementary school again. Although, these elves are striving to attain a better attitude about these things than we had previously. But really, elementary school again?

So also there are those who are ready to awaken to their elfin natures and those who are not ready to do so. Often elfin feel frustrated that someone they love and admire simply doesn't understand their attraction to living the Life Elfin. But some are simply not ready to do so, and in fact, it may never be their path. Just as you can explain how a car runs to your dog or cat or pet bird, it doesn't mean the dog will understand. You can only share on the level that the individual Spirit is upon at a particular time. It is rude, of course, to *talk down* to people, to speak to them in a superior fashion, but it is ever important to communicate on the level that they can understand without any judgments, even judgments suggested in tone of voice or body language, about the level they are upon. They are where they are, and if you are going to lift them up you must reach down to that level, or stage of development, to do so; and even then they may not be ready to grasp the offered hand, or may not even notice it is there.

It is not that this is an intellectual path, which is not to say there are no intellectuals who tread it, but it does not require great knowledge or education to be an elf. It just requires that one pursue hir own nature and the path of evolutionary enlightenment with sincerity and joy. Any faerie child happily singing and running about in the joy of a spring day can evoke Faerie/Elfin, and certainly do so far more profoundly than those of us caught up eternally in our own thoughts, worries and concerns.

Yet, we also need to understand that Karma and Fate hardwires our propensities into our brains. If a person is not ready to awaken they cannot do so, except under extreme conditions of stress, desperation and danger, or these states mimicked shamanically by imbibing certain tree or plant substances, with repetitive drumming, dancing and chanting that create trance states. For these states release this synaptic hardwiring and allow it to be rewired under new conditions. Also, near death trauma, that is to say suddenly getting near the Source, can affect this profound change in individuals.

Yes, we know that seems paradoxical and is in many ways the opposite of what we said previously about arriving at the place of serenity and avoiding stress and how stress keeps us from Elfin/Faerie. But, the Quest and its challenges are made to produce just such situations that can transform us. It is after the Initiatory Quest that the Path of Serenity opens. The first Quest, the frequently stressful quest, is the quest to find Elfin, even when we didn't entirely know what we were searching for, which usually means our elves find us. The second Quest, the quest for serenity, is about staying in Elfin, about being able to endure on the path and not fading back into the world. Remember always, even when we are not directly searching for Elfin, that is we are searching but are not exactly sure about what it is we seek, our kindred are ever on the lookout for us.

And while not everyone will call thems'elves elves, or define their path the way we do, every individual is seeking the fulfillment of their own Spirit, and every Spirit, whether Elfin or not, who is on our level or a similar level is one of our kindred, whatever sHe chooses to call hirs'elf, or however sHe understands hir spiritual quest. Anyone who is following hir true path to hir true s'elf without harming others will always be considered one of our own by these elves. Our question is not: do you agree with us, but do you wish to be our friend or not? Among the elves the words friend and elf are almost identical in meaning. To say that someone is an elf-friend is to say sHe is elfin as far as we are concerned. We see the elf in everyone. However, it would be rude to call someone an elf if the individual chooses to define hirs'elf in some other way. We ever respect the right of the individual to declare for hir own s'elf what sHe truly is, even if that definition is only a temporary one.

Vibrational Understanding

It would be nice if everyone who called hirs'elf an elf, was a developed Elfin Spirit, but that is simply not the case. Even among the Elfae, there are those at different stages of vibrational attunement. The more advanced the elf, however, the greater will be the elf's ability to harmonize with other elfin, as well as all other beings. This does not mean that those others will see or understand the elf other than as a rather pleasant seeming person, or that they will necessarily advance more quickly thems'elves, although Great Elfin Spirits do have a tendency to have an invigorating and empowering effect on those they encounter.

However, those who are close to such a Spirit, either in physical location, or in vibrational resonance, are more deeply influenced by such a Spirit. The first group of individuals are influenced because, since they are in physical proximity, they tend to encounter the Great Elf frequently, which creates a subtle but profound effect on the person over time; and the second group because, being developed in their own s'elves, they are already open and receptive to such a Spirit no matter how far the distance between them. Thus, the more advanced Elfae are ever in communion with the Shining Ones, those great evolved elfin, who abide in dimensions that are often far removed from this one.

This vibrational attunement is a form of knowledge. Those of very close vibrations of a higher level immediately understand each other forthwith, with little if any need for words between them. They need not even speak the same language; their shared smiles communicate all that needs to be said. Those of a less advanced vibration also often understand each other, but usually tend to see each other as competition, or have the attraction they feel for each other obscured by their selfish passions and drives. The old saying: too many cooks in the kitchen, rather aptly describes the effect these have on each other. (Note: we elves tend to make a distinction between selfish and s'elfish. The first seeks personal gain regardless of the needs or concerns of others. The second, s'elfish or 'elfish, seeks the fulfillment of hir personal goals while harmonizing with the needs and cares of others, always striving for a win-win situation.)

Enchantment

So it is easiest for those of an advanced Spirit to awaken Elfin, but even awakened they still must develop from the level they happen to be at the time they awoke. It is not wise to expect too much too soon. It is true that we enchant others at times, or that some become enchanted by Elfin for a time, but in our experience this enchantment in which the individual seems to suddenly function far beyond hir previous capacity, is only inclined to last for about a year, and then the enchanted Elfae fades back into the world and usually wanders off into new fads, and quickly returns to the vibrational level sHe was functioning on at the time of becoming enchanted.

There is no harm in this, however, except in so far as the elf who created the enchantment is often surprised, chagrined and may feel a certain bit of loss when the one they so loved fades away. Yet, for the individual so enchanted, this relatively brief sojourn in Elfin creates a memory secreted deep in hir unconscious of the magic of Elfin, and more than likely sHe will encounter the vibrational energies of Elfin again and be drawn to us once more. Only this time, hir experience and awareness will have increased, and sHe will be more deeply affected by the Call, and will usually stay for a longer Spell and may even continue on the Path permanently, for this second brush with Elfin plays upon the first experience, is thus more profound and reaches more deeply into the Soul. And the fact that the individual has faded and returned is, in itself, an indication of an increased Spirit and Soulful vibrational development.

Know Thys'elf

The Sages tell us that the path to knowledge begins with knowing our own s'elves. We begin by knowing our lower s'elf, our passions, drives, and desires, and when we remove from these our prejudices and dark spells of enculturation that lead us to s'elf and other destruction, we are essentially left with our own attractions and interests. These, of course, may change, so we need not assume that we are our attractions, anymore than we are our opinions. We are ever and always pure being. But in trusting our attractions and gaining experience by way of following the path they suggest to us, we develop our Spirits and become, what we always were and are, our own true S'elves, only with increased power and vibrational energy.

If these attractions are not us, however, what are they? They are the Call of the Soul, and our link between our consciousness and all that is about and beyond us. Our attractions call us out of ours'elves, that is call us to extend ours'elves either outwardly or inwardly, both of which directions extend into Infinity. Space, which does not exist but Is and thus allows existence, stretches out forever in all directions, including inwardly. It is a paradox of Elfin, and the elves realize that Paradox is at the heart of Creation. Most people refer to that paradox as the Mystery. It is the Mystery that Mystics are ever endeavoring to contact and commune with. It is the Mystery that Scientists ever seek to understand and explain. But no matter how much they learn and explain it, it just seems to present them with more questions, more mysteries. And it is the Mystery that unfolds in the heart of Faerie.

So who are we? We are whoever we wish to be. The key here is Wishing. As the faery tales tell us, one of the great powers of the Elfae is the power to grant wishes. So, beloved, what is it you truly wish? Who do you truly wish to be? Your own true s'elf, of course, and how you define that will depend upon your actions, which is to say your magic. We create ours'elves in everything we do. Think about that. Every action we take helps shape our life, our karma, and our destiny. Make your actions meaningful and your life will be filled with meaning. Make your actions magical, and you life will be filled with magic. Have your actions be a true reflection of your inner nature, and your life will be filled with power of your magical being, your true s'elf.

Yet, unlike so many others, we elves are not inclined to talk about what we are in a definitive fashion. Our definitions of elves in general and ours'elves in particular are ever open and transformative. There is a world of possibilities that we include, and there is little that we exclude except prejudice, cruelty, and robotic behavior. Elves may be of any race, any nationality, ethnicity, or social level. Despite how images portray us, we are not of any particular physical type, although we are inclined keep ours'elves in shape and to take good care of our bodies. Elves are not necessarily even human, or humanoid, there are tree elves, avian elves, and elves whose bodies are but light and ether. It is difficult to define us because we are ever becoming. But what one can say about us is that we are ever seeking to be our best, do our best, and increase the power of our personality, the awareness of our consciousness, the health of our bodies, and the harmony of our associations. We seek to develop our skills in all our pursuits and endeavors, knowing that every advance in our powers will benefit us, and all others.

This is the intertwining of our Spirit and our Souls. We seek the best in and for ours'elves, our Spirit, and we seek the best for all our others, our Soulful connections. As we become increasingly aware of the unity of these aspects of our being, we also become increasingly attuned to the Realms Beyond, from which all knowledge comes, particularly those hints that lead us to further initiation and success throughout the dimensions.

We, each of us, desire success, which is the power to achieve what we will in the world or realms we inhabit. This success can be defined ultimately as Happiness. We cannot do this alone. We simply cannot. Some may think they can do so, but that is an illusion as long as we seek that success in the world. If we seek success utterly within our own s'elves, and needed nothing from the world, are content with all that comes to us, then perhaps we can find success alone. But our interaction in the world, our need to succeed there, is itself an aspect of Soul development, for all that is beyond the boundaries of what we are as a Spirit can only be contacted via our Soul. Some may ignore its higher impulses, and thus also lose the benefit of ecstatic awareness that comes with this interaction, but to go beyond ours'elves, to succeed in the world, requires Soulful interaction.

Interestingly, the Spirit by its'elf, that Spirit that finds success within its'elf and finds contentment in its Soulful connection to the world about it, attracts luck and success to its'elf. Contentment attracts contentment. Thus the best way to attract success in the world is to develop one's own nature and be content, that is vibrate happiness, in as much as possible to all beyond one's s'elf.

It is true that there are certain lower level Spirits who are so Soulfully challenged that they despise all that is happy, innocent and pure. They seek to destroy it, and one must, or perhaps should, be aware of a need to protect one's s'elf. However, it is important to understand that the reason they seek to harm the innocent is because they are really endeavoring to silence the pain and madness within their own beings. They really wish to be purified; they truly, although they don't realize it, want to regain their own innocence; but as yet they just don't know how to go about doing it. They hunger to be transformed, but like so many who are unhappy with their lives, they seek to change it by trying to change their environment or by changing those around them. Alas, they will never find self transformation out there. It is really their own selves, or that part of themselves that haunts and drives them mad that they really seek to destroy. They seek power and control because they feel inwardly powerless and out of control.

Knowing this truth, the elves do not vaunt our happiness. Our contentment is quiet, subtle, and compassionate. To most, we are ever unseen. We can blend easily into the world if we so desire; but we can also be the anomaly that is so out of the ordinary that others convince thems'elves that they did not see us at all as soon as we leave their presence. All that is left is a lingering sense that something special occurred, but they can't quite remember what it was.

We are also aware that often we are but actors in other people's dramas. For most people, their expectations define us. They see us as they assume us to be, based upon their past experiences, their prejudices and their desires. Most of the time, we simply allow this. We use their expectations to our advantage, furthering ours'elves without harming them. But sometimes, we must clarify ours'elves for them. We come into sharp contrast to what they were expecting. And this is often difficult for such individuals, for they do not give up their preconceptions easily. So wherever possible we allow them to keep their assumptions, and we work our magic around them. It is far more efficient that way, and only when necessary do we force them to truly see us. This can be a shock to them, and even having seen us they may, and will most likely, revert back to their preconceptions in short order. And in most cases, that is just fine. After all, we were only bit players in their drama anyway.

But at times, if we encounter these folks again and again, we must reorient them. This can be a bit shocking to them, so much so that in some instances the effect can be as profound as a transformative trance experience. Then they may see the world anew, or become enchanted for a spell. Still, people do no change easily, or quickly, or if they do change suddenly it seldom lasts for long, at least this tends to be the case for positive changes. Most things that change suddenly do not do so for the better. True positive change must be earned, and that takes time. And we must always proceed from where we are at the moment, and until we learn the skills for stepping from one parallel world to another, transformation comes very slowly. And even in dimension hopping, it needs to be understood that the worlds are very close together and interwoven, so even under those circumstances the alternations in one's life and world may be very minute, at least at first. Only the adept will notice the subtle differences.

Agreeing to Agree

We elves often agree to disagree. The fact that people have different opinions than us does not bother us. Opinions are opinions after all, and little more than dandelion fluff floating on the wind. We make wishes upon them as they pass by. Each has the right to pursue hir own Path in hir own way as long as sHe doesn't obstruct the true path of others.

But we elves also agree to agree. We set aside opinions for the common good and work together toward mutual goals and seek to understand each other. We don't tend to argue, we are not much for criticizing. If our opinion is requested about how something may be improved we will give it, but we don't seek to idly tear things down just to make ours'elves seem clever, as so many seem determined to do in the modern world. In elven society, if you think something can be better, then it is your responsibility to try to make it better. It is not enough to say something is bad, or inadequate, you must offer a better solution, or seriously set yours'elf to discovering, or inventing one.

Our agreement to agree is a pact to help each other improve ours'elves in all that we do. Our society is a society composed of individual Spirits, and the health and welfare of each individual reflects on the success of society as a whole. We help our others as best we may, for this helps us and makes for a more harmonious Elfin. We are individually and collectively One in our Souls with Elfin/Faerie.

Of course, for some this is all too Airy-Fairy. It seems like fluff to these individuals as they look out into a hard, cold and potentially dangerous world with villains seeking our doom and plotting against us from nearly every direction. And we understand that. We have no problem with those elfin warrior Spirits who seek to defend us from the dark sorcerers of the world. Many a brother or sister elf has spent time training in the military. It is not beyond the conception of these elves that one of ours might aspire to be an Army Ranger or Navy Seal, or other elite warrior. What after all was Legolas? We are ever saddened, however, although not surprised, when there are those who think our aspirations toward a greater connection to Spirit and the Soul of Elfin, and our Vision of a more peaceful world, is fluff. Endeavoring to lead a peaceful life and to delve into the higher dimensions of esoteric reality takes a great deal more courage than most realize. There are few who have the courage to take on the wicked of the world head on; there are even fewer still who are courageous enough to enter the Perilous Realms of the psyche and see thems'elves for who they truly are.

Beloved, the current conflicts of this world are a seeming, an illusion, born of the Karma of the Past and carried on by Karma into the future. The circumstances of the world will pass only to be replaced by more of the same in endless repetition until we, through the integrity of our actions/magic, transform this world into one more prone to harmony than conflict; and that will only happen as we transform our own Spirits and Souls into ones that are Just and Strong, Powerful and Compassionate.

Of course, there are those who think the world is as it is and will never change. And perhaps they are right. After all, it is we who do the changing, not the world, and as we transform ours'elves we will step from dimension to dimension getting ever closer to that Radiant Realm we call Elfin. We do not seek to deny you your world of conflict, if that is what you insist upon having, we merely wish to offer you an alternative.

Parallel Worlds

We live in the Ever Present and Eternal Now. That is reality and that is the true nature of time. All that could be is now. However, since it cannot all be in the same place, it is spread out in space and exists in its most subtle form as energetic possibility. What most people think of as time, the phenomena of change, is really movement of our consciousness across space.

All these possibilities that exist Now, create parallel worlds or dimensions that are interwoven and linked to each other. Those that are most similar are closest to each other, those dissimilar or opposite, are further apart. Every time we make a decision, we subtly step from one parallel world into another. Because the worlds are so close together, they tend to be only marginally, fractionally, different from each other, so for most decisions we've made we don't even notice the world has changed. Usually, only very small things have transformed, something is there that wasn't previously, or something has disappeared as though it never existed. You, in fact, may be the only one who remembers it.

In choosing to live our lives as elves, we step ever closer, one world at a time, toward Elfin. The more these choices become an integral part of our Spirit/Soul the more profound that change becomes, and the less likely that we will step back again. Like someone giving up smoking or drinking who then relapses, there are many who make progress toward Elfin/Faerie only to fade back toward the world as they lapse into old habits. But also like giving up smoking or drinking, one can find new resolve and each time one strives again one gets closer to the goal.

Know who you wish to be as a Spirit, live that life as best you can, and even if you relapse occasionally, know that the Way is ever open to you. You can always begin again, renew yours'elf, and in doing so grow ever closer to your true S'elf that is your true destiny.

Doubts

The world as is appears solid and real to us, as it is meant to be, just as dreams seem real when we are in them. And they are. The shaman knows that all things are real. This world is real. Dreams are real. All we experience is real. But it is not always as it seems to be, and there is always so very much more.

This world is an illusion, not because it isn't real, but because it is only a part, a very miniscule part, of the True Reality. As Spirits we are limited, and it is only in connecting to our Soulful natures that we can go beyond ours'elves and have a true sense of life.

Let us explain this again. All things are real. Lies are real lies, falsehoods are real falsehood; artificial sweetener is real artificial sweetener. Everything is real, but not everything is as it presents itself to be.

Naturally, we develop doubts. There is so much that is and we have come to understand to be really false. There are so many who are out to deceive us, and even those who are sincere don't always know what they are talking about. They heard it somewhere, they read it somewhere; they're taking it on faith and passing it on to us. The same is true here. We are telling you what we have come to understand from our own experience, and our own reflections upon what we've encountered and been told is true in the world; it is you, however, who must contemplate these things for your own s'elf, and decide what is true for you. Every elf will understand that that last statement is indeed the Truth. You must decide; because you are shaping and creating yours'elf by choosing your own direction through the realms and finding your own path, and thus accumulating the experiences that mold your being.

Doubt, while valuable, however, and necessary, can get in the way when we explore the inner worlds. At first it has importance, one needs to examine one's experiences to sort out what is valid from what is mere wishful thinking or fantasy projection; but there comes a point when, after having examined oneself thoroughly that one must come to trust the s'elf and one's inner perceptions, as well as one's imagination, for the realms we explore communicate through the imaginal. And there is significance to and reason for the imaginings toward which we gravitate. Again, there is a reason for the attractions we have, and progress is slow and painful indeed when we struggle with ours'elves over every detail of our being. Once having glimpsed the greater Reality, we need to at least have faith that such a Reality does indeed exist, otherwise we become stalemated going over the same experiences again and again. Yet, nearly all of us have done so at some period in our development as we've wavered between the Call of Elfin and the insidious insinuations of the World that seek ever to create doubt.

Having felt the Call of Elfin and having responded to it in one's heart and Soul, one needs then to pursue the path fully and not forever stand on the near side of the Mists constantly asking one's s'elf whether what one heard was truly the Call of Elfin or not, and whether indeed there really is a place, dimension, actual state of being, that is Elfin.

To find Elfin, we must open ours'elves to its vibrations, becoming innocent but not naïve, strong without being callous, knowledgeable without pretending to be all knowing. Ours knowledge needs to be an open knowledge, a knowing that is ever ready to transform its'elf, just as we are ready to transform ours'elves, as new experience and information expands it. We are ever in the process of Becoming, for we are part of the Great Mystery, and we are perfect and perfecting ours'elves at the same time.

Where do you go from here? That depends on you, on who your are, where you are, and who you wish to be/become. While our experiences help to define us; and others, often eagerly, wish to tell us who we are to them, only we can decide by our own actions who we are truly. We shape ours'elves in all we do. For we are elves; and we are a magical people.

And whatever direction you choose to take, whatever you do, remember true change takes time/space to become integrated into one's being. On the other hand, we have Forever. And our more advanced kindred are out there always, sending us magic to help us on our way. Are you sending magic to those out there who are also searching?

And remember, dear kin, whatever your conception of yours'elf in its most powerful and successful manifestation is a mere shadow of what you are truly destined to become. You will be so much more than your wildest ideas about yours'elf. But that is far, far from here and we are just taking another step, and another. The high mountains of spiritual development seem so far distant that it may appear at times that we will never reach them, but we will, and on climbing them we will see there are endless mountains beyond. There is no rush, really; we have a long, long way to go. And if we find each other on the way, and tell tales of our adventures by the evening campfires, and camp down together beneath the shimmering stars, secure in each other's company, then what can be better than that?

Out Of Our Minds

Most people we encounter in the modern world think we are joking when we tell them we are elves, or figure we are caught up in a Role-Playing Game, or some other fantasy, and if realization comes to them that we really think we are elves, they then assume that we are crazy. And we acknowledge that we may be. But a pleasant kind of crazy, an eccentric kind of crazy, a loving, kind and magical crazy that so many secretly admire but are too afraid of social censure to dare to be.

And the truth is in order to find Elfin/Faerie, we have to be out of our minds, out of the ever doubting, analytical mind that picks everything apart, dissecting frogs to see if there is a Soul inside, and not finding one, concluding that it must not exist. To find Elfin, we must get out of our minds and come to our senses. Or really, we must open our minds to the awareness of our sense/Soul feeling and follow that feeling, like a metal detector as we heed the Call of Elfin within.

It takes a fair bit of courage to pursue the Elven Way. It takes a good deal of Spirit development. One cannot be forever concerned with how others see one, forever in need of their approval, for at this point in the journey, one is unlikely to get that approval, and in fact one is very likely to receive a good deal of disapproval, criticism or down right rude reactions and ridicule, even from those one thought to be one's friends. For most folks at this stage of evolution, the Elven Way does not garner the sort of respect that might be accorded to one if one told others that sHe is a Buddhist, Hebrew, or Christian, although, even these have their detractors. It is possible that the supra-dimensional path will never be accorded that sort of respect, except by one's fellow aspirants. One must be strong within one's s'elf to be an elf, those of weak Spirit will ever endure upon this Path.

But even if we were accorded such respect, it would only mean that in being a socially acceptable path, that many would come to it who are not really ready or not sincere in their aspirations, and in fact, in some instances this already occurs due to the popularity of J.R.R. Tolkien's *The Lord of the Rings*. But that does not bother these elves, or the Shining Ones who guide us. Many will come to the path, wander into Elfin unaware only to wander out again when another fad calls to them. But none who enter Elfin/Faerie go away untouched. Faerie dust, the shimmering radiance of our realms, will cling to their souls and no matter how far they wander afield there will always be a bit of Elfin within them, calling them back. Not all who come to us stay with us, but all who come are meant to do so even if they don't stay for very long.

The Great Mystery

The mystery lives within and beyond us. It exists in all things, for are not all things a mystery to us really? We endeavor to understand them, but they are always so much more than the definitions we give them. As the General Semanticists say, it is unwise to mistake the map for the territory, and the territory is ever changing, especially in Faerie.

Who are we really? We are not our thoughts, our passing emotions or our transitory feelings; we are not our bodies, or our opinions, in particular, we are not our opinions about ours'elves. We are a mystery, even to ours'elves and we are ever endeavoring to solve that mystery, to understand who we are. We are pure conscious awareness, even when in fact we are not always conscious of our consciousness. Yet, we are conscious even when we seem not to be, which is to say there is a level of consciousness that exists beneath the thoughts that are generally mistaken for awareness. Becoming aware of ours'elves, becoming aware of our awareness, becoming conscious of our awareness, puts us in touch with our pure potentiality. But it is our actions, our magic, motivated by our Spirit that defines us as unique beings. As pure conscious awareness we are One with All. As beings of magic, as Spirits, we are One with All Uniquely.

The Great Mystery lives in all things. It lives within us and beyond us. It unites us all and seeks ever to understand itself as we each become aware of our true s'elves, and as we Become, by way of our magic, and our experiences. We know, this is not easy to understand. But then, it is a mystery. And mystery ever calls us to quest. To quest for knowledge and understanding, to try to figure it all out, to solve the riddle, puzzle, mystery. The mystery is Elfin/Faerie and it ever calls us to become our own true s'elves and by searching to understand the mystery, within and beyond us, we are drawn to the experiences that shape us.

We are not one thing stagnate and unchanging, we are Spirits ever evolving. Our true s'elves are not this as opposed to that, or here as opposed to there, but rather this becoming that, and here on the way to there; which will be here when we get there. We are energy in motion, defined not by where we are but by our trajectory and the tone of our vibration. We are eternally becoming and always our s'elves. Being our s'elves and becoming ours'elves at the same time.

True Knowing

Most of what we know, or think we know, is merely ideas, facts, and opinions. Even much vaulted scientific knowledge is not absolute and is subject to change as more data comes in and more effective theories, that is theories that more closely fit the facts, are established. Things that we truly know are born of our experience. However, even then what seems true is only a point of view, an interpretation of what happened. Several different people can experience the same event and all have a different point of view, a different experience, as to what took place.

This is in part true because in a very real sense we all live in different parallel overlapping worlds. We seem to be in the same world because our worlds are so interconnected and similar, but they are each marginally different from each other. Connected, yes, overlapping, yes, but not exactly the same. We, as we said, each have a different point of view, a different perspective of events. Each experiences the world in a different way from a different perspective.

Two things tend to moderate this. First, social agreement inclines many individuals to accept a general view that has been promulgated so the individual sees things, experiences things, as hir enculturation has programmed hir to view them. This is the fact for the mass of individuals in the world, and they experience what they expect to experience. Anything that violates that expectation is either soon dismissed and forgotten, or so profound as to send them into a state of shock or traumatic reaction. It is just this traumatic reaction that the shaman seeks to invoke through hir techniques of ecstatic realization. It is just such shocks that appear as enlightenment, the sudden discovery that there is much more to the world/Universe than one previously thought. And it is just this sort of shock that often occurs when one has wandered through the Mists into Elfin/Faerie and awakens to the realization that it is indeed real.

However, the adept takes the second course, since in most cases sHe has already passed this event long ago. Having cleared hir mind and hir being of expectations, and approaching life with an open mind and a pure heart, sHe sees things as they are for hir. That is hir experiences are direct and real, although still hir experiences and, still from hir point of view. SHe has a greater and more accurate view of Reality, but it is only as sHe expands hir Spirit through Soulful connection that sHe begins to perceive a more expansive and thus more accurate and inclusive view of the Real. The more we can view the world from other beings' perspective the closer we come to reality.

And in gaining this higher view, we also begin to perceive the Supra-dimensional realms where the Shining Ones abide. We begin to enter Elfin and see not just one world, but worlds interwoven. We begin to understand others as Soulful Spirits, that is as they understand thems'elves to be and more than that we begin to see their potential, and in seeing that potential can then call to it. In this way, we begin to attain one of the Truly Great Powers, the ability to bring out the best in everyone we encounter. And as this power develops, those we meet will be inspired. They will feel a need to do their best, be their best, to be the best person/Spirit/Soul that they can be.

To know the truth within ones'elf is to arouse that truth in others. The clearer we become as Spirits, the more in touch with the Truth of Reality, which is infinite possibility, the greater our Spirits will grow touching more and more Souls without any effort to do so at all except our own effort to be our own true s'elves. It all comes round to this again and again: you are a mystery unfolding, becoming all it wills to be, shedding all that obstructs it, and in so doing unleashing your magic in everything you do.

Calling To Faerie

Having heard the Call, the elf naturally responds, calling back to Elfin/Faerie, seeking it in one's heart, reaching out with one's Soul, hungering for it with every fiber of one's being. What does the Spirit do? It acts. It searches for others in the world, and other elfin can be hard to find at times, particularly advanced elfin, or elfin on one's own level of development or close to it. The yogis suggest we seek "right company", but right company can be difficult to locate sometimes.

Alas, finding bad company or inadequate company seems all too easy. Clearly, we must avoid company that would lead us astray, but also we must be careful of hanging out endlessly with those who are, at this point, merely spinning their wheels in the world. These are not bad folk, but neither will they help us toward our goal of magical realization and enlightenment. There may not be awakened elves about us, but our friends need to be true friends, sincere friends whatever their spiritual path. Which means, in part, that while they may not share our path or the understanding of our pursuit of it, they have to be open enough to acknowledge its genuineness for us, just as we respect them on their path.

As we've said previously a true friend is an elf friend to the elves. We do not seek to convert others to our "faith", although we are always eager to share our culture with those who are open to it. And we trust that others will not endlessly seek to convert us to their faith. Yet, we are ever open and curious about other's practices and beliefs, particularly their magical, which is to say in many ways, spiritual practices. We are ever eager to learn about their relationship with Spirit and spirits. But who of us is not delighted when we find our very own? We ever seek others who share our magic and our understanding of the realms, those that can help us on the Path, share with us the Way, and be our companions in friendship and love as we explore ever more deeply the realms of possibility and magic that we call Elfin.

We are ever seeking our own true kin, but as always, the best way to find them, and the best way to find the best among them, is to be our best, to develop our own Spirits; for an illuminated elfin Spirit is a beacon to all who seek Elfin.

Creating the Atmosphere

It is also important, however, that we create the right atmosphere for Elfin/Faerie, the right vibration, a magical ambience that is attractive to Elfin, both the state of being and the beings of that state. First, or perhaps simultaneously, we do this within ours'elves and then, and at the same time, around ours'elves. We live the life elfin within and without.

Our desires create affinities and these affinities attract us as we attract them. In pursuing our desires with whole hearted action our actions and desires tend to become one. We become magnets for what we desire, although in less developed Spirits not very powerful magnets. Many hunger for power, or money or sex who do not achieve it; their Spirits are not developed enough to do so. Yet, still in desiring these things we are attracted endlessly to them and pursue them with fervor, our minds and Souls become filled with them. And in time, perhaps not this particular lifetime, but in some lifetime to come, we will surely achieve what we so persistently pursue.

In just this way we must pursue Elfin, hungering for it with our whole hearts, opening ours'elves to its vibrations, surrounding ours'elves with the attractive ambience of and to its nature, and most of all being open to the changes to our own s'elves that will occur because of this pursuit. Just as someone who desires sex must strive to make hirs'elf attractive to those sHe desires, so must we make ours'elves attractive to the energies of Faerie. And what is Elfin/Faerie attracted to? Magic woven with Love and Starlight. Faerie is the realm of enchantment. To attract Elfin we must become enchanting; we must be enchanters.

It is true that you may need to hide your light. To let others assume about you what they wish to assume, keeping your elfin nature hidden from all but your inner circle, or those you reach out toward in the hopes of establishing such a circle, having a secret sanctuary that exists if in no other place than in your heart and Spirit and Soul. You may need to live your magic secretly, weaving spells unseen with gestures unrecognized, sigils invisible, and enchantments cast from your mind, but live your Elfin life you must, if you are to call Elfin to you.

Still, the best of all worlds, as every Elfae knows in hir heart, is to have other Elfae with whom to relate on a regular basis. And elves together functioning as a unit are a power indeed. Still, while a group is more powerful than an individual (usually, except for very developed Spirits), it is always individuals that must compose it and the devotion and development of these individuals is vital. The more advanced the Spirits who participate, the greater the power. So make yours'elf great. Improve yours'elf in every way you can, develop your Spirit, attune your Soul, listen to the Call of Elfin and call back through your devotion to your magic. Remember, the more developed you are as a Spirit, the more powerful you become, the more attractive you become to your others, drawing your others to you as surely as you are drawn to Elfin.

But Calling to Elfin is a step beyond hearing the Call. The Divine Magic is ever awaiting us and Elfin is open to all who are sincere in their approach. But one must approach. We not only need to make ours'elves open to the influences of Elfin, but we need to activate these energies by our own lives. We resonate them in our own magic. It is not enough to wait for something to happen. Or it is enough but it may seem to be nearly forever before anything occurs. We elves are a magical folk. We don't merely wait for Elfin to come, we don't simply look around for it in the world, we don't, although this is very important to do, only seek it in our own s'elves; we create it day by day. We take what we find of magic and our elven culture and we make it real for our own lives, transforming it so it works for us, and our others. That is the Elven Way, and in pursuing it, we find that all that we've been seeking comes to us through our own powers of creation.

Dealing With the Gods

As we've said, these elves don't worship any Gods or Goddesses, although we know a few living Goddesses and Gods that we very much adore. They are truly wondrous beings, utterly adorable, we can't help but love them. It isn't a choice we make, and surely there isn't any doctrine involved; it is instead a spontaneous wonder that is evoked by their presence. Their Divinity shines forth, and even though they are still human beings with their own particular frailties and foibles, none-the-less, they are a marvel to behold; the Divine manifest on Earth so clearly and profoundly. Yet, as we've indicated, we don't worship them, except with the love that springs unbidden from our hearts.

Besides the Living God-desses we encounter, there are the traditional Gods, too, the Gods and Goddess of this or that religion. We treat all these Gods and Goddesses with respect as well, even though we are not followers or devotees of their particular sect, cult or religion. But that is our basic policy in dealing with all Spirits regardless of whether they are more, or less evolved, than we, or on the same level. Not all beings have earned our respect, but all deserve recognition for the Divine within thems'elves. Part of what we do as elves, part of our magic, is seeing the Divine in others that they do not, as yet, see themselves.

But as we've pointed out, while we believe in all the Gods and Goddesses, we don't necessarily believe what their own followers tell us, or what they believe, about them. Gods and Goddesses are not all the same, although like us they come from the One Source, and they are all on the evolutionary path of development on various levels of adeptship and in various dimensions of beingness. All life is subject to the underlying urge toward S'elf/Spirit fulfillment, even those beings so often accorded to be Gods. And, it should be said, compared to us in power and development, they are Gods; only they are still not as powerful as many would have us believe.

Now, most folks in the world, even most elves in this current era, have come from a religious background of some sort. There are, also, agnostics who retain a scientific objectivity and reserve the right to wait until some real proof arises as to the existence, or lack thereof, concerning Gods, but there are not many of these. And there are Atheists who deny the existence of Gods altogether from what is essentially a materialistic viewpoint. But most folks come from a religious background of one type or another, some more traditional or fundamental than others. And even those who have released their belief in a particular religious dogma still embrace an idea of God overall and many still hold affection for the religion of their upbringing even if they no longer believe in its teachings and tenets. So we hope that if you are one of these you will not be offended by what we say next. We are, after all, merely expressing our view concerning the world that works for these elves, you have every right to believe as you do, and we intend no insult toward any particular God/Goddess or religious group in revealing our own opinion concerning some of the more popular Gods and their supporters.

From our understanding, Judaic-Hebrew peoples were originally a pagan people who in coming into contact with the Egyptians, who were descended in part from civilization we call Atlantis, took on their Gods, particularly Amon-Ra. The Atlanteans had been in contact with, and influenced deeply by, the Annunaki Shining Ones, those inter-dimensional travelers who came, as legend tells us, to Earth and tinkered with anthropoid DNA, mixing it with their own genetic makeup to create more intelligent beings. In time, they came to be seen as Gods and ritual worship was established in the memory of human contact and relationship to them. It was they who rode Chariots of Fire (space ships or inter-dimensional portals) and so deeply influenced human development. We don't ask you to believe or disbelieve, we only suggest you contemplate these ideas.

As the Bible tells us the Judaic-Hebrews, as often happens with immigrants, came to be suppressed in Egypt, whose civilization had declined from the higher teachings somewhat, so the Jews fled from this oppression into the desert where they made a covenant with a Djinn, or desert spirit that lived on a local mountain. He was, as we are told, a jealous God/Djinn/Genie/Spirit and gave those people a set of rules, ten commandments, the first of which was that they should have "no other gods before Him", which is to say he was to be their chief God always. It does not say, as so many interpret it to mean, that there are no other gods, or that their god is the only god, just that He was to be their God. It was a pact of mutual exclusivity. They worshiped Him alone, and He looked after them and no other people.

This Djinn is essentially an elemental spirit, powerful truly, but not all powerful as some believe, and also on his own evolutionary path of development. He is an evolved Spirit, but not one, we think, that has as yet actually been a human being. That development will come in future rounds of evolution. At the same time, we should note, that esoteric Judaism, as revealed through the Qabalah, has a deeper understanding of the nature of the Universe that is not dissimilar to our own experience and understanding. When we speak of the Djinn elemental that has made a covenant with the Jews, we are speaking of Exoteric Judaism. And again, we don't mean to offend any of our Jewish brothers and sisters, we are simply giving a different view, an elven magical view of "Gods".

Out of Judaism arose Christianity, which tells us that they, the Christians, are also followers of that very same Djinn who had a son, Jesus, through spiritual intercourse with a virgin. This formula, of the god-child, half-human, half-god, who comes as a hero to save us, is sacrificed and born again, was a not uncommon formula of the ancient worlds and is reflected in the Osiris-Horus mythos, as well as in the life of Pythagoras and others. This is the same formula of the sacrificial king who renews the land with his blood.

Alas, the Djinn of the Jews, having made an exclusive contract with the Judeo-Hebrew people, had no interest really in

Christians. Thus, we find that most Christians, while giving lip service to that ancient Djinn, really worship his son, Jesus, the half-god, who like Perseus, was another son of God who came to save humanity. You can see reflected in this formula both the notion that humanity, or part of humanity, was elevated by the Gods through intercourse with them, thus reminding us of the Annunaki and their intertwining with humanity, and the idea that, as Jesus tells us we are all children of God and can also become aware of our own immortal natures.

However, we also see Jesus, who in our minds was clearly of Elfinkind, as an advanced Adept, who obtained union with his immortal nature and rose by doing so into the higher dimensions. Of course, in due course, as so often happens, his teachings were turned into a religion than only marginally reflects his Spirit, and most of those, but not all, who claim to be his devotees haven't the faintest clue about what those teachings really were, and even when they are passingly familiar with them, still do not follow them.

Similar in many ways is the story of Buddha, who was also a human being who achieved adeptship and rose on his own merit. Of course, we can make a case for Buddha being related to the gods as well, or half-god, half-man, since in ancient times all kings and their progeny were considered Divine representatives of the Gods on Earth, and from this arose the idea of the Divine Right of Kings. Since Buddha was a prince he was thus descended from the Gods. This also follows the myths concerning the Holy Grail, the Royal and Divine Bloodline of the Elven Peoples that Laurence Gardner illuminates in his books. But still, whether fully human or half-god, Buddha proclaimed an essentially scientific method of enlightenment, which was really, if you look at it closely, not entirely different from the scientific enlightenment espoused by Scientology. Scientology uses technology, the e-meter, while

Buddhism used meditation as its primary tool. This is a very loose comparison but we think, in essence, a valid one.

Buddha, having obtained enlightenment, moved on to the higher dimensions. Those who were left behind, as so often happens, formulized his teachings into a religion. This is really a common practice and is a way of making the higher teachings accessible to the masses. They are watered down for those who are not quite ready for a heavier doze of the truth. And we should note, there is not simply one Buddha, but several, each having obtained enlightenment, or Buddhahood, and usually then spreading his particular formula into a new land for a new people. From this has developed various sects of Buddhism. These elves are fond of Buddha and honor his wisdom greatly. But, like the Christians, Buddhists also interpret the teachings of their god/sage according to their own tribal/national background and culture. People may change their religions from time to time but changing their own selves takes a longer span of evolution. Again and again, well-intentioned and positive religious doctrines will be reinterpreted according to the prejudices and customs of the tribes that adopt them.

Islam, on the surface, would seem to follow the same God as that of the Jews, but of course, the Moslems do not. They do, however, relate to a similar, and related Djinn from another desert mountain. It might seem that the Djinn of the Jews and the Djinn of the Moslems hate each other, but we don't actually think that is so. They are relatives so they may have a tendency to squabble, as so many relations do, but they also love each other. They are family after all. However, you must remember that these are Djinn, Genies, very powerful but still directed by those who let them out of the bottle, so to speak. They each have a commitment to their followers, and when their followers come into conflict with other groups, often due to ancient tribal rivalries, they have no choice but to get involved. And naturally, they take any threat to their devotees, their power base, very seriously.

Of course, the older the religion, the less likely it is to have fanatical followers. Moslems may kill you for drawing a cartoon of their prophet, Mohamed, praise be his name, or making fun of their religion; but Jews, for the most part, could care less about what any foolish outsiders, such as these elves, think about them. Christians tend to be in the middle. Old Christians, such as Catholics don't like being ridiculed, who does, but are unlikely to get overly excited about it. Evangelicals, new Christians, are a bit more on the touchy side. However, as a general rule the more mature the religion and the devotee, the less they care about what others think about their faith. And no matter what you say about their religion, Buddhists just seem to smile knowingly.

We should note that both the Hebraic-Jews and the followers of Islam allow no graven images of their God, which is a reflection of the fact that at the heart of each of these faiths there is an understanding, particularly by the esoteric scholars, that their God comes from the Source, which is pure and undifferentiated energy, and for which all things are possible. The tendency to anthropomorphize this energy into a human-appearing being is a reflection of two aspects, the dilution of the teachings to make them accessible to the common devotee and the fact that when the God appears to them he sometimes takes on a human-like form, albeit one irradiated with light. We will speak more on this in a bit.

Taoism, which originally began as a sort of back to the land movement not dissimilar to those hippie Taoist of the sixties and seventies, with their go with the flow, revel in nature attitudes, also has been turned into a religion with its eight Taoist Immortals. These are also said to be humans who attained enlightenment, but in many ways these are really archetypal energies, that is the driving forces of humanity, immortality, longevity, health, prosperity, etc. given expression as seven Gods, and one Goddess. But essentially, Taoism is a form of nature magic, and is in many ways not much different in its pure form than modern Western Wicca. These elves, and most elves, are a very Taoist folk, although not as a religion but as a magical philosophy.

Hinduism is not one religion but many mutually tolerant religions and is very much like modern western Paganism with its worship of Pan, Odin, Zeus, Cernunnos, Hecate, Diana, and all the other and various Gods and Goddesses. Krishna, in some ways, stands out as another prince, like Buddha, who achieved enlightenment, godhood and rose to the higher or more subtle dimensions. Most of their Gods/Goddesses, however, are devas, or angelic spirits who have already evolved though lifetimes of manifestation, through all the forms of evolution, such as animal life, as many of their Gods indicate by their animal forms.

There are, of course, many, many other religions on the Earth and surely beyond it, that we won't go into here, but for the most part all of them worship Gods that are either elementals, like the Djinn; illuminated and elevated humans, such a Buddha, Krishna and Jesus; devanic spirits, who are also elevated humans, but from ages past; or animal spirits, that is the Spirit of the Divine as it manifests in various animal forms. This really covers the progress of evolutionary development for the most part from mineral life, Djinn related; animal spirits; human adepts; and devanic-angelic spirits who have evolved through the cycles long past. This includes the Shining Ones who are the guides and mentors for the Elfae.

There is certainly nothing wrong with relating to various Gods or Goddesses if you don't evoke them in order to do wrong anymore than it is wrong to receive help, guidance and protection from one's parents, elder brothers and sister, or cousins. There is a certain point when we all need such help to progress, but there also comes a time when we must come into our own as Spirits, although not necessarily alone. Realization and enlightenment may be a gift to us from those more enlightened, but like healing, it is something we must make our own. Others may offer us healing, but it is we who must heal. Our brothers and sisters of the Way can help us with guidance and assistance, and Elfin may call to us, but it is ever we, as individual elven Spirits, who need to devote ours'elves to our own development, our own magic, if we are to achieve the Way. This hunger for illumination, for s'elf realization and knowledge of our Immortal s'elves must burn brightly in us and turn all lesser desires into the minor flames that they truly are.

Why Good Girls Like Bad Boys

As we've told you, humanity, Spirit, Soul, and Life have certain underlying tendencies and drives such as the Quest for Life Eternal and the Quest for Happiness Everlasting, symbolized by the Two Trees of Elfin. But from these are many associative aspects that are also favored genetically, which is to say if you have any of these aspects developed in your Spirit you are most likely to get laid in DNA's effort to produce more of this favored energy. This includes success in various forms, beauty, intelligence, cleverness or genius, and certainly courage and daring, as well as, an exciting personality.

This is why good girls and bad girls like bad boys. They tend to be courageous and daring and that is a very appealing quality, favored genetically, and illustrated in such sayings as fortune favors the bold or brave. Of course in time, many of these bad boys fail to develop other favored qualities, like financial security and success, and as time goes on girls mature into women and change their attitudes about what qualities they find appealing according to their needs at particular age.

Our point, however, is not that you should be daring if you are not so disposed, but that each of us needs to develop the talents, qualities and propensities we do have to the best of our ability, and in as much as possible to take those aspects in which we are weak and improve them as well, even if only a little bit. This is easier for things that we desire. That is to say if we are weak and desire to be strong (another favored quality), we can exercise to become stronger or more muscular. However, if we hate math and don't want to learn it, while it is good to improve our skills in everything, our reticence may also be telling us that this is not the path for us at this point. There is nothing one cannot improve in ones'elf if one practices consistently and ever seeks to improve one's ability; however, there are things that for whatever reason don't call to our Spirits or our Souls at a particular time, and if fate doesn't compel us, or our path lead directly to it, there is no need for us to pursue them. You, after all, are a free Spirit, you must choose what is the right course for you. On the other hand, if fate puts us in a situation where we have to do or learn such things, it is also best to do our best; for as we've pointed out previously, it makes it easier. If we don't resist, and we embrace our circumstances, we can always use them to further ours'elves and our elven sorcery.

We must each look at ours'elves objectively, to come to Know Ours'elves, as the Sages advise us, to know our talents, skills and weaknesses and to do all we can to make ours'elves better, to rid ours'elves of those weaknesses, and increase our ability and strength in all ways, always. Easy, no, not necessarily, but easier as this becomes a habit of our being, and easier still as we gain in power, hone our skills and enhance our abilities. The great power, however, as all Sorcerers know, is the Power of the Personality, the Power of Spirit development, particularly when the Power of the Personality, the Power of Spirit, combines and unites with Soulful realization, which is to say a compassionate understanding of others. Then the Way opens, and Elfin pours into our lives, magic happens, and the world, which is a reflection of that magic, becomes ours.

Magic Happens

Tolkien pointed out in his scholarly article *On Fairy-Stories* that the magic of Faerie and thus of elves and faeries is not the same as the magic of most magicians and sorcerers. It is not a labored attempt to manipulate circumstances around us, but rather stems from our natures and the nature of Elfin/Faerie itself. Our magic stems primarily from the power of our personality, of our Spirit development. It is more in the form of enchantment than intentional manipulation, although we do indeed cast spells now and again, however, they tend for the most part to be generalized evocations of luck rather than of manipulating specific circumstances.

Most of the magic that occurs around the elfin is actually spontaneous, arising impromptu from the effects of our personality/Spirit upon the world. It comes in the form of Synchronicities, meaningful coincidences that arise, in our minds, because our luck/magic/Spirit calls to us the fulfillment of our Will. An elf need do no more than develop hir own s'elf and magic/enchantment will begin to arise around hir. And the greater the Spirit development the more powerful and frequent becomes this confluence of synchronicities. Nature, the Universe, and the Supra-dimensional beings with whom we associate, whom we call the Shining Ones, act on our behalf shedding their own light and magic upon us.

Some of we elfin love magic in all its forms. We are occultists, esotericists and adepts of the magical arts and study the techniques from all peoples and cultures in the world. However, this is not at all necessary for the elven. Each elf charts hir own course toward S'elf realization, hir own path on the Elven Way, and no elf needs to be a magician, sorcerer, or witch for magic to occur in hir life. SHe needs only be and develop hir own S'elf and the magic will flow to hir (and through hir), just as iron is attracted to a magnet. Of course, all elves are naturally enchanters but this springs not so much from spell casting, although we do cast spells, but from the mysterious and intriguing quality of our personalities.

Mayavirupa

As we develop our Soulful Spirit, and rid ours'elves of the passions, prejudices and other aspects of our lower selves that bind us to our current human bodies we also become lighter in Spirit. One can work to intentionally develop their higher body, their astral body, their body of light, but even if one doesn't practice the exercises to do this, the clearing and purifying of the personality, the strengthening of one's spirit, and the illumination of one's soulful connections will have the effected of enlightening the Spirit and thus the body.

As we become more light-filled, or as Reiki practitioners would see it, filled with healing or Reiki energy, or as we elves tend to view it, filled with the radiance of Elfin, we become closer to our supra-dimensional s'elves and thus increasingly able to move into those more subtle realms of being and realization.

This does not, however, preclude us from interacting in the mundane realms of manifestation. Even those beings, or perhaps, particularly those beings who have developed in the supra-dimensional realms, realms we call Faerie, are able to travel to or through the worlds most of us currently inhabit. They may even appear to us, if they so desire, using a Mayavirupa or energy/light body that appears human-like, or like an animal, or whatever form they chose.

This is how a supra-dimensional God-like being, like the Djinn of the Christians can impregnate a human girl and still leave her a virgin. In a material way, we might think of this as a mixing of DNA, but really it is the mutation of DNA when it comes into contract with a Radiant Being of Light. Just as nuclear radiation will cause genetic mutations, so does contact with these beings, although in a more positive fashion. Thus did the Annunaki or the Nephilim interbreed with proto-humans and alter our DNA toward greater intelligence as well as instill in us a hunger for the light. The more elfin we become, which is to say the more we develop our Spirits, our true natures, the more light/radiant we become, and thus more attuned we become to Elfin/Faerie that radiant dimension of Enchantment.

Meeting Ones'elf

Jung said that most folks cannot see their own Shadow self because it is so hateful or obnoxious to them that they project it outwardly on others. Thus in war the enemy is projected as an evil empire and not simply another group of individuals who oppose us and seek success for themselves at our, or others, expense.

So, too, most of us in striving toward higher realization often ignore our lower impulses, dismissing them, or really hiding them from ours'elves just as we attempt to hide them from others, in the same way we hide our bad habits from someone we are courting. We like to make a good first impression, be on our best behavior, etc. However, under stress these aspects of our s'elves often come out and we are suddenly confronted with our anger, greed or lust, or other aspects that inhibit our development.

Naturally, such realization of our own inadequacies, particularly when we thought we had evolved so far beyond them, are a painful thing to us; but it is important to realize that such revelations of our nature, while difficult to face, and exasperating due to the stress involved, are in fact a gift, from the supra-dimensional beings who guide us, to reveal to us those parts of our being that we still have to work upon. It's not easy to say, "thank you," for revealing to us that we really are assholes at times; and usually such thanks is only offered later when we've actually made some progress in terms of eliminating these obstacles to personal development and thus Mastery and Power; but truly such things are put there to help us, although that is not easy to see at the time, and these elves react to them probably as you may, with "Oh, shit, not again." There are great Spirits who eagerly seek out stressful situations in order to hone their spirits, and these elves applaud them. Alas, we are not there yet. We prefer the slow way, dealing with stress when it does occur as best we may, and avoiding it as much as possible most of the time, while none-the-less ever seeking through daily s'elf examination to purify ours'elves and develop as Elfin Spirits. We elves tend to seek the easy way, the path of least resistance, which takes much longer but is oh, so much more sure, and certainly less stressful.

At the same time, struggling with one's s'elf tends to have one forever entangled in one's faults. It is far better in the long run for the most part to note one's tendencies, observe them, as one observes thoughts in meditation, which is really what they are, passing thoughts manifesting as reactions to stress, and instead applying one's s'elf to putting energy into the positive aspects of one's s'elf. In this way in time, these positive tendencies will become far greater than the negative ones, which will then disappear. At that point, one no longer reacts to stressful situations by struggling with them, anymore than one struggles with the thoughts that pass through one's mind as one mediates, but rather one very simply applies one's s'elf to taking action in a step by step fashion to solve the riddle presented by such circumstances. We wish we could say we have totally mastered this ability, but alas it is not so. We, perhaps like you, still strive to perfect our elven natures. Yet, this is also true of the great Shining Ones, as well, on their own level of development and realms of manifestation, although certainly in much more subtle ways than we. The Path is never-ending.

The Humanity of Gods

So it is that those who guide us are also on the path of evolutionary development and perfection. This is true of those who many think of as Gods as well as those less powerful and less perfected Spirits who sometimes appear in our lives to aid and guide us.

It is sometimes shocking to those who have followed a particular faith to realize that the individuals they thought of as perfected beings, are in fact, quite human after all. Many people lose their faith when this happens. These elves have known more than one kindred to convert to Christianity or some other faith because of the charisma of a particular preacher or group of devotees only to find out that they didn't really live up to the ideals they espoused. We have also encountered those who profess to be high adepts who are far less evolved, far less powerful and far more human than they presented thems'elves to be.

We, however, have come in time to appreciate this fact. We prefer our guides to be able to understand our level of development, and we find that while we appreciate the wisdom and guidance they offer us, we *love* them for their humanness, that is to say their foibles, and for their elven-ness, which is to say their eccentricities and unique aspects of creative personality. They are beloved to us not only because they mentor us but also because they are such unique and wondrous personalities filled with quirks and aspects of personality that we find quite lovable even though at times they may be irascible. When we are honed by the friction of personalities clashing, it is not only we who are shaped thereby. You do your mentors no good if you but meekly follow them. Someone needs to speak truth to power, and often it is the elves who do so. Although, we are also wise enough to know when we just need to keep our mouths shut, and our thoughts to ours'elves. It is not our fault if those who are sent to guide us are not wise enough to learn from us as well.

Some decades ago some of the guiding lights and philosophers of the Elenari came to visit these elves, and they graced us with the opinion that we were very advanced elfin Spirits and expressed the hope that someday they might be as advanced as we. We let them know that one: they were far more advanced than we were when we had been their age, and two: that most of what they presumed to be us was really their own light, aspiration and future, reflected upon us. They weren't entirely seeing us. but rather they were seeing thems'elves as they wished, and would be in their future. They were projecting their own light and vision upon us.

These elves don't choose our guides because they are perfect; we choose them because they offer us the information, knowledge, skills, techniques and wisdom that can further us on the Way, and even though they are not always, or seldom perfect as Spirits, they are none-the-less quite amazing elves.

Over-Shadowing

Sometimes the greater Spirits, or the Great Soul, speaks through us. We radiate our own light that has been enhanced by the Radiance of Elfin. So also, as in the case of the Elenari seeing their own future potential in us, we project our own light on others that we presume to be further on the path than we. Although, it is good to remember that if we are seeing them they can't be too far distant from us. This projection of the light happens in many ways in the same fashion as the projection of our shadow on others. But sometimes the greater Spirits do inspire us. We are uplifted by the Spirit of Elfin as we become increasingly attuned to it, and as our Soul/Spirit becomes one with its Soul/Spirit.

This is also the case when others, often schizophrenics, get messages from the lyrics of songs, or from someone's writings, etc. Haven't you experienced it? Haven't you read the *Lord of the Rings* or some other novel and felt like they were talking about you? Describing in many ways, your life? Of course, it is not the author/writer speaking to us. They are not aware of us at all. But it is the magic speaking to us. It is often Elfin speaking to us through our psyches via the writings. Of course, in some sad cases, usually with poor tormented schizophrenics, it is wicked little demons that are speaking to them, and sometimes they are aware of this fact, and at other times not. It really all depends on what the message is, and whether it urges you toward the realization of your Soulful Spirit, or toward the destruction of yourself or others. Messages from Elfin will always call you to the development of your true s'elf, and urge you soulfully to aid others on this path as well. Messages from the Elvish Realms will ever tend to increase your awareness, awaken your elven nature, and guide you toward those acts that will increase your power without accumulating negative, thus painful, karma. In reading our books some may think that we are very advanced elves, but really it is your own potential greatness, your true s'elf that is inspiring you. We are but wee folk really, and if we are a bit farther down the Path, it is not all that far really; you will catch up to us soon we have no doubt. And honestly, dearest, we can hardly wait. We will have such a good time when we eventually find each other.

While this process of radiating the Light of Elfin in our lives is traditionally referred to as Overshadowing, it is really more on the order of Inner Illuminating. It is not a process, as in Voudoun, of being ridden as a horse; it is not trance mediumship where a foreign entity takes us over for a time and we have no consciousness or memory thereof, as is apparently the case with Ramtha. By the way, we are making no judgment here. Whether this is a good thing or not depends upon the spirit who overshadows the individual and the individual hirs'elf. That is to say is sHe a willing channel or not? Channeling the Light of Elfin is, instead, rather like having the sun shine on you through the clouds on an otherwise overcast day; you appear all the more brighter thereby but this radiance is added to your own, it does not overtake you, you do not lose your own light (although it may indeed be overshadowed, that is seem dim in comparison to this greater radiance), nor your consciousness or awareness. And just as others get messages from a book that the author didn't specifically intend, so do others see the Light of Elfin according to their own level of development and their own needs at that time. In serving Elfin, we are ennobled, rather than being mere tools for the intentions of greater powers.

Sexual Attraction

Sex is one of the primary desires that face most of us, most of our lives. Elves, for the most part, love sex, however in its lowest form it, too, needs to be mastered, and it is by mastering it that this drive is elevated. It is important that we don't allow our sexual drive, which is connected to both our drive for immortality and our drive toward happiness through pleasure, to control us. And, as most mature elves know, it is only when we obtain some real mastery over this drive that we really begin to "get some". Mastery, adeptship, is sexy. It will get you laid. The more advanced one is in hir elfin nature, the more sexually appealing one becomes. At the same time as the lower aspect of sex attraction is transformed, it turns into an attraction for those who desire mastery, adeptship and spiritual realization, in other words, those on the Path, and is perceived by others as spiritual beauty and illumination. This is in part why worldly power and position are such powerful aphrodisiacs.

One of the keys to mastery of the lower sex drive, which involves experiencing the drive without necessarily acting upon it, and not as some may think an extinguishing of the drive altogether, is the basic aspect of Friendship. Mature elves always establish friendship, mutual respect and affection as their base for all relationships, including and particularly, sexual relationships. Before sex, during sex, and after sex, we ever wish to be friends.

This does not mean that we should ignore our natural attractions. These attractions, as we've said previously, are extremely important, but things seldom turn out well if friendship, mutual elfin respect, is not part of the relationship as well. On the other hand, the same is true of pursuing the path with devotion and getting involved with someone sexually, even though one is not really or entirely attracted to them, just because they share the same path. We have done this, and it does not turn out entirely well. We have in the past become involved with someone sexually, merely because sHe was also manifesting as an elf, even through we didn't find hir attractive. This proved to be a mistake, although because we did this out of a devotion to the Way, great benefits also accrued. But it was a mixed bag.

The same is true of getting involved with those who are not on the Path but who are physically attractive to us. We may have sex, but the outcome is seldom satisfactory in the long run. Most important, always, is the sharing of mutual respect, friendship and affection, and this requires a certain level of maturity or mastery. It is far better to get involved with someone who isn't of the path, but with whom we share a mutual attraction and sense of friendship, than to be involved with someone who is temporarily on the path, but who doesn't have the maturity to carry on the friendship when the sexual relationship has ended. But best always is to get involved with those on the path who share friendship, attraction and mature development. Combining our passions with the Way empowers the Magic.

So it is that there are those, often of a mystical inclination that eschew the body and its needs and concerns, thinking that by denying the body they will enhance their spiritual and soulful development. Perhaps this is so; however, it is not the Way that most elfin would choose. We are not here to separate ours'elves from our bodies, or from the world entirely but to master and transform them. We do not neglect our bodies, abuse our bodies, or deny their needs. We do all we can to improve ours'elves in all ways, including our appearance, health, and strength; and to fulfill our bodies' needs and drives in a positive and healing way; and this certainly includes the fulfillment of our sexual drives, which Elfin/Faerie in its wisdom so often uses to guide us in the direction we are meant to go in, although, obviously such drives can lead us in the wrong direction as well. How do we know the difference? We ask ours'elves, is it healthy? Does it further us on the Path to Elfin? Does it harm ours'elves or others? And is there the magic possibility of friendship? Subject your sexual proclivities to these questions honestly and you will find the path that is right for you. Sexual attraction, when mastered and when guided by the principles of the Way, can be a great oracle for the elven, for as we say it links the body, and the feelings to our goals of Life Eternal and Happiness Everlasting, which when interwoven manifest as the primary theme of Elven Life: … *And They Lived Happily Ever After.* This very simple, common and traditional Fairy Tale Ending is a Great Formula of Elven Magic.

If we are not harming others or ours'elves, then the path or relationships that attract us (which for elves are often the same thing) are most likely a safe path to tread. If it is good for us, healthy for us, and if it increases the possibility of friendship, then it will surely draw us closer to Elfin. And if it involves enchantment and romance without violating the previous conditions then it is bound to be magic; and elfin magic stays with us forever. Even if we become senile, get Alzheimer's, or die and pass from these bodies, we will always remember those we have loved, those with whom we have shared romance and elfin magic, in the deepest core of our Souls.

Consider this before sleeping with someone: everyone with whom we have sex will be connected to us Soulfully forever. Forever! Our mind may forget them, but the memory will never be erased from our Soul. On the other hand, blessed kindred, we are on the Path to Elfin, following the Elven Way, and it will all turn out to be magic in the end. The magic turns all things to its advantage and there is no wrong it will not eventually make right, no wound it will not eventually heal, and no heart broken that will not be mend by wondrous love.

The Separation of Spirit and Matter

And remember, while some spiritual disciplines see a dichotomy between matter and the spiritual realms, we elves do not. The Divine exists in all things and lives in potentiality in matter, which is merely energy in a very organized or structured form. The Source is far more protean, that is more adaptable and flexible; in fact, infinitely so. And the closer we get to that Source, the more flexible and adaptable we become; or the more flexible and adaptable we become the closer we get to the Source. Remember, inflexibility, or rigor mortis, is an aspect of old age and death. If we would be Immortal we must become ever more adaptable and flexible. Rigid and inflexible individuals hasten their deaths. They stand against the movement of the Universe, against change, transformation and Becoming, and they are eroded and washed away. It is true that the supra-dimensions, and the beings that inhabit them, are closer to the Source than we, and technically speaking they may be more Spiritual Beings, although that is not always the case; but even so that does not mean that matter doesn't have the spark of the Divine in it, only that those realms are more illuminated and more protean, that is to say have greater possibilities of magic and the instantaneous fulfillment of our wills and intentions than the mundane world usually presents us.

In a certain sense, it is a matter of protocol. The supra-dimensional beings, being adepts of great order, have less protocol to go through to enact their wills, the mundane plane of existence is far more structured, or more form oriented or protocol oriented, and there is often far more steps to go through to get what we want. This mundane world is really a huge and cumbersome bureaucracy. As we get closer to Elfin/Faerie, the realms will be far less inflexible and we will experience far more freedom. Of course, what you do with that freedom depends on you, and some enter there only to set up their own bureaucracy and thus entangle thems'elves in the mundane realms once again. But let's face it, freedom can be terrifying at times. And most of us, at some time or other, call out to the Shining Ones to guide us.

The World Is One

It is important to remember that the Universe is One. The Supra-Dimensional Realms, where our bright kin the Shining Ones abide, are not separate realms from our own, not really, anymore than the ultra-violet and infra-red spectrums that we can't usually see without equipment to do so are separate from us, or the invisible radio waves that are nearly everywhere on this planet are separate from us. We don't usually perceive them, but they are here.

So, too, Faerie/Elfin is here, all around us, ever and always, it's just that most of the time, most of us don't see this realm anymore than we see ultra-violet. However, as we become more attuned to those dimensions, as we become more Elfin by following the Elven Way, the more apparent those realms become to us and we see them manifest all about us. Elfin/Faerie overshadows this world, so to speak, or really inner illuminates many of its denizens; and when we gain Elf Sight through contact with Elven energy, the depth of its relation to, or penetration into particular areas and individuals, becomes ever clearer to us. We see gnomes, and leprechauns, elves, brownies, dwarves and all manner of folk, even when they don't realize these aspects in their own s'elves, just as a writer may carry messages in hir work unknowingly, as we pointed out earlier. Elfin magic makes use of everything; and it weaves its way into all things that are in the slightest way open to it, which is to say in which the Spark of the Divine Magic flares even in an infinitesimal flame.

Contagious

These elves often chant: Healing is contagious, Pass it around. This healing energy is elfin magic; and elfin magic, and the Elfae nature its'elf, is contagious. Just as vampires, in the stories and legends, past on their nature through the sharing of their blood, so do we elves pass on our natures, or really the desire to realize one's true s'elf, by sharing our magic. Which, because our magic is derived from our characters and personalities, our Spirits, happens naturally whenever anyone associates with us for a length of time. The more one hangs out with Elves, the more one tends to feel free to be one's own s'elf. It's only natural. The Divine calls to the Divine in each of us. Elfin/Faerie ever calls to its own and to hear its Call is to awaken our Elfae nature as it stirs within. We do not hear the Call out there, although it may at times seem quite distant, we hear it within.

Elven Blood

Some see our race as being one among many human and other races. This is not how these elves see things, but we do acknowledge that the myths, legends and tales of elves and others stem from, or were more strongly influenced by some tribes than others, and that there are those who are descend, as we are, from these tribes (For more on this read Laurence Gardner's *Realm of the Ring Lords* or Nicholas De Vere's *The*

Dragon Legacy or even the *Story of the Irish Race* by Seumas Macmanus). But as you develop as an elfin Spirit, one also comes to see that world of Spirit does not originate from the material world, but quite the opposite. The material world arises from the Realms of Soul and Spirit. They are interconnected, really One thing, but the origin of the world is the Source that is Pure Conscious Awareness in its aspect of Infinite Possibility and Energetic Being. All else is form and variation of the energy/consciousness as it fulfills possibility with thought and thus structure or differentiation/variety.

And while there are those among the otherkin who claim they are not human, this is more an aspiration really, a desire to separate ones'elf from the madness of mankind, than a genetic actuality, although, non-human Elfae surely exist. We all come from our ancestors out of Africa, and before that from what is commonly called Atlantis, and before that Lemuria/Mu, and before that Pangaea the united continent, and before that from the stars, which is to say the more subtle dimensions. All people really are descended from the Shining Ones who interwove their light with our DNA and transformed us. Not all of us are destined, or choose, to call our s'elves elves, or Elfae or other, but we are all destined to realize our true s'elves. The more elfin one becomes the more one realizes we are related to everyone and everything. And this is a good thing. It is the way to Mastery and Power in the Universe, which is mastery and power over our own s'elves. The more expansive that understanding of s'elfhood is, the wider is our reach. We become, as they say in common parlance, "connected".

What makes us elven is not so much our blood, or our genetic lineage, but our Spirit that chooses this Path. Nearly every culture, every people in the world have tales of us, for every culture stems from, and comes from, the same Source. But not all of us are going in the same direction and not everyone hears the Call to Elfin/Faerie as we do, or calls Elfin/Faerie by that name, or sees and experiences it as we do. But all will find their own true s'elves, the development of their Spirits, and in as much as we respect these differences, we are Soulfully connected. As we elves say, there are many paths through the forest and it is vast and ever growing. Unlike the forest of this world that are fast shrinking, the forest of Spirit continues to expand. Elfin/Faerie grows wider and deeper with every Soulful Spirit that awakens to the realization of hir own true nature.

Our true bodies are made of light. We are not so much elven bodies, but elven Spirits, yet as we become more and more our own true s'elves, that is as we come to develop our Spirits, the lighter we become and our bodies physical and our Spirit will be One Light Shining amid a Universe of Stars.

We are not elves because of our elven blood, or genetic heritage; nearly everyone on this planet has a bit of elven blood in them. The world is filled with those of elven blood who do not hear the Call as we do, and do not choose to pursue the Elven Way. It is not our bloodline that makes us elves. In fact, no one makes us elves, but us. We are elves because we choose to be elves. This is an act of Spirit, of Magic. This is an enchantment, and we are the enchanters.

However, because the mundane world is born of the Source that is the Magic, our acts, our choices not only affect our future, which is to say our fate and karma, but it also slowly transforms our DNA. Just as a choice to smoke or not smoke, drink or not drink, will affect one's body so, too, does our choice to pursue the Elven Way affect us. Those who live the Elven Way (we could say pursue the Elven Way, or follow the Elven Way, but live is a more accurate understanding of our Path), become more elven. While the elven nature tends to atrophy in those who do not *live* The Way. This is not a judgment on them. They also are destined to realize their true nature, but in their own Way, their own Dimension. Ever, we bless them on their Path. And if we can help them, whatever their choice of Way, to awaken to their true nature whatever it may be, we are ever eager to do so.

The Swing

Our Spirit body is Light, literally, and thus very flexible, protean and resilient, while our mundane body is dense, slow to move and change (comparatively) and at times tends to resist the actualization of the light body. There is reason for this. We have descended into matter in order to learn to differentiate and define ours'elves. But now the time has come for us to take those lessons and return to Elfin, the radiant realm of our Immortal S'elves.

This movement from our mundane body and its natural but lower, or reactionary and impulsive drives, to our Body of Light with its elevation of our drives toward Power and Mastery creates a back and forth movement, rather like a swing that is reflective of the Ying and Yang of the Tao, the seasons within seasons or Nature, the fluctuation between energetic movement/activity and rest, waking and sleeping, and much more. So, also, we make progress toward Elfin and toward our true natures, and then we slack off. The harder we drive toward Elfin, the greater the slacking off when that cycle comes. We hear the Call, and then it seems we hear nothing; and then we wonder did we just imagine it?

This is, of course, quite natural. In fact, it is the way of Nature and what seems often to be a circular movement, going around and around again and getting nowhere becomes, as we progress, a spiral; going around and around and slowly rising, by keeping ours'elves attuned to our goal within. This takes

Spiritual devotion and aspiration, although it first tends to arise as a Will to Power.

The mundane body senses its immortal nature while seeing, when it is filled with consciousness, the transitory nature of its form. It instinctually knows that the energy that composes it is eternal, but that its current structure will pass. Thus the basic drives toward Immortality and Happiness/Pleasure arouse the lower self to aspire toward Power and Control over its self, and its environment. However, these early attempts at power generally overshoot the mark and lead, as the body is so often inclined, toward excesses of various sorts. We become absolute hedonists, drug addicts, tyrants, control freaks and much more. All of these are but lower, in most cases early, attempts to elevate the s'elf.

The usual reaction is to give up or try harder. Prostitutes become religious converts, drug addicts exercise strict control over their s'elves, tyrants become wild anarchists, and wild anarchists tyrants, and control freaks become depressed and feel out of control. It all swings to and fro.

As we develop ours'elves, however, as we gain slow but sure mastery over our natures, these swings become less extreme and this brings quicker progress with less disruptions. Instead of fighting ours'elves and our natures, we come to know ours'elves, and we work with our natural tendencies. We strive when we have energy, we rest when we are tired, we follow the Call when we hear it, we call to others when we do not, relaying the Call as we are meant to do. We understand that Nature flows and ebbs, and we attune ours'elves to this realization. Thus we do not batter ours'elves against immovable walls. We begin to understand that all that happens is leading us to Elfin and our true natures if we but use every event and circumstance to develop our Spirits and our Souls. The world as it appears to us is an illusion, which doesn't mean we don't felt pain when it strikes us but that we use that pain to further ours'elves. The

Pain is transitory, the Path Eternal. In that way we become like the Magic its'elf. Just as Elfin/Faerie uses all things to its advantage to further its goals and Way, so may we use all we encounter to hone our Spirits, and in doing so we become ever more attuned to Elfin and therefore ever more attuned to our own s'elves. We share Elfin's Power, and we become Magic. It is not so much that we do magic with labored effort, but become magic, so everything we do is magic. Easy? No and yes. It is as easy as we make it, but the more attuned to Elfin we become the easier it is to attune to it.

Every action creates an equal and opposite reaction. If we do not resist the swing as it moves backward, we increase our power when it inevitably swings forward again. And that is the point. We must come to understand that all things function under these Laws of Nature and the Universe and adjust our magic to move in Harmony with them. This begins as an act of faith, but in time it becomes certainty as we observe Life and Nature, and come to understand and feel its rhythms and its "moods". Just as we must adapt and adjust ours'elves to the mood swings of individuals with whom we live, or with whom we share a relationship, so it is wise to realize that we are in a relationship with Nature and with Elfin.

Alas, the relationship with Nature can be at times a hostile one, particularly since so many are so hostile and uncaring of Nature. We elfin, naturally, endeavor to woo Nature, to get in Her good graces and to live in harmony with Her, and this greatly benefits us. We are blessed due to this, and for most elves this results in aging less quickly than most non-elven folks are inclined to do. We look younger longer and we have a propensity, for the most part, to be younger longer.

Our relationship with Elfin is somewhat different. Elfin ever seeks to woo us and when we respond with openness we are additionally graced with light, magic and power, particularly in the form of knowledge, wisdom and understanding. Our movement toward Elfin is ever a dance. We step forward, we step backwards, we sway side to side but we never lose awareness of our beloved, and our beloved always is aware of us, enchanting us ever more deeply toward that realm where Love is Realized in Radiant Wonder.

So this is all to say, there is no need to despair, dear One, if you yearn for Elfin, you will find it. In fact, as we've said, in yearning for it, you've already taken the first step toward it. In yearning for it you have signified that you have heard its Call. And while it may seem at times that you've lost sight of it, lost the sound of the Call, lost faith that it exists at all, it is still there and will Call again. We know there are kindred that are lost out there, and we have come to find them. You are surely not one of them or you wouldn't be reading this book. If you are reading this book, not just glancing through it, but perusing it, then you are already far on the Path to Elfin, and the realization of your true nature. Let your light shine, dear kin, it is the Light of Elfin as manifested by your own nature.

As to those who have lost their way, who have come to Elfin and faded again, or have sought but lost hope that they will ever find Elfin, or that it even exists, they are not reading this, but we will find them as well. They've not read this book as yet, and may never do so, but we are also coming for them and will lead them home again, as long as that is where they truly wish to be. See you back home.

Effortlessness

There is a Zen aspect to our Path, we are magic and thus all we do is magic; it happens automatically, as a result of our nature, just as breathing does. Yet, we still do magic, that is intentional magic, but it is never a forced or artificial thing. It stems from the needs and circumstances of the time, and thus is quite natural as well, like having a meal when one is hungry and needs nourishment.

We elves, for the most part, prefer to do things the easy way, to take the path of least resistance, because this is also the most energy efficient way to do things. In this way the swing changes from a huge movement back and forth to the spiraling circular movement like a crystal on a string going round and round. Some folks, of course, prefer this huge back and forth movement, and truly the greater the swing goes one way, the greater it goes the other. These folks are often called Manic-Depressives and one finds many of them among the less developed elven. The manic phase, particularly when it is creatively oriented, can feel great and be incredibly productive, but the depressive phase can be devastating, even suicidal.

And yet, what is the alternative? The alternative is to pursue with steady devotion one's own attractions and creative pursuits. If we are forced to put effort toward something we have no interest in really, we will tend to resist and this resistance will make it more difficult. If we force ours'elves to pursue things we think are good for us but which also lack the vital aspect of attraction, it will also prove to be a trial, although we may drag ours'elves through it anyway. However, when we pursue our natural interests, whatever they may be, under the guidance of the admonition to Harm None, then the energy we put toward this pursuit doesn't exhaust us but tends to empower us. Inevitably the body will need rest, but the Spirit will be energized and the Soul nurtured and magic will become easy. We will go forward naturally with hardly any swing back, and no resistance.

So, whatever it is that turns you on, as long as it doesn't harm yours'elf or others, and as long as it furthers your Spirit and your Soul, is a good thing. Your natural interests and attractions are inherent in you and exist for the very reason of Calling to you; and when you involve yours'elf with them creativity then they energize your life, and help you on the way. Obviously, if you are but a consumer of your interest, you will not make as rapid progress as you will when you become creatively engaged in it. But, the avaricious consumption phase, that is buying, collecting, reading, viewing all in your field of interest, is a common first stage of any Quest, and is part of the process. First, we must familiarize ours'elves with the territory and get to know all we can find out about it. Later, having filled ones'elf with all there is available, one will want more, and will search farther afield, seeking the rare and the esoteric, and eventually one will realize that there is still something missing, something one will never find in the world just by searching. And that thing is one's own creation, one's own contribution to the field. When you make that step from consumption to creative participation, you begin to enter the realm of the Initiates.

Although, it is also true that sometimes we pursue one interest, consuming all we can learn about it, only to get bored and have it lead us to another interest. This is also natural, although some parents get frustrated that their child was determined to learn the oboe (or some other instrument or interest that cost them dearly) only to abandon it in due order. But this movement from one interest to another is part of the path, and while we may not immediately settle upon that area, or areas, that will eventually be our true focus, everything we learn will in time be of value to us. The Universe is a connected whole and everything we learn supports our understanding of it.

So, beloved, pursue those things that interest you, even if others make fun of your pursuit and think those interests immature or unworthy. As long as you are not harming yours'elf or others, it's none of their business anyway. Integrate all you learn into all you know and use your interests, and the knowledge and energy you gain thereby, to further your s'elf and your personality. In this way the Path becomes natural and easy, actually wonderfully enjoyable, learning becomes automatic, and one cannot but, through the course of time, discover and develop one's own true s'elf. Be yours'elf, make your magic effortless and thus be energized by it.

Magic Costs

There are those who always say, Magic Costs, and by this they usually mean, you will have to sacrifice something for it, someone will have to die, anything good that happens will cause something bad to occur, etc. This is only partially true. All movement requires energy that is true; but Magic, the Quest for one's own s'elf, is an investment. Yes, one must put energy into the Quest, but the dividends will be enormous in the long run for those who remain devoted to the development of their Spirit.

Something good happening, doesn't necessarily mean something bad will happen to balance it out. Have you noticed them saying the opposite? That when bad things happen, greater good shall come to you? Well, sometimes, if you pray to their chosen God. It really depends upon Karma. What sort of karma did you accumulate in doing, that is to say, living your magic? Make your magic natural, requiring no extra effort, stemming from the light of your Spirit and Soul, and what you will attract is more magic, what you will cause will be Light, and it will come to you by way of Love.

Such fearful admonitions to avoid magic usually come from those who are, indeed, afraid of magic, which means really afraid to trust their own s'elves. Often, these are individuals who used magic in a destructive way in the past and who now cling to the guidance of a particularly evolved spirit, whom they like to think of as their, or everyone's, God. And for them this fear of magic is a good thing. They are not ready to use it again, which also means they are not yet totally trustworthy. In the face of such as these, elves often hide our light, letting our magic appear to be but an aspect of a Role Playing Game or a fantastic imagination. It is true that there are some who are also frightened of these as well, thinking them Satanic, and around these folks we must be even more cautious, for they are not to be trusted at all. They have given up magic, but they as yet haven't given up the tendency to want to interfere with other's lives and to control those around them.

Of course, this stems from the fact that deep within they feel very out of control and they are trying very hard not to lose control; but we elves know the tighter they hold the reins on their Spirit, the more it will eventually rebel and we don't want to be around when they eventually, and almost inevitably, "lose it". So from these folks we tend to fade almost entirely. We do not let them see us for who we really are at all. "Magic?" We say to them. "Don't be ridiculous, there's no scientific proof for magic. You must be joking!"

Everything Furthers

When we live the Elven Way we treat other beings with respect and courtesy. As we grow stronger as Spirits, that is more confident in ours'elves and our personalities, and thus better able to interact with all manner of folk, we also become more Soulfully aware. Although, we could also say that the more Soulfully aware we become the greater our capacity to positively interact with others, also the more attractive we become. We become less inclined to judge people, less inclined to separate ours'elves from them out of fear, and more inclined to nurture them, often in very simple ways, such as a nod, or a smile.

This is not an automatic skill. It is unlikely that we will wake up one day and find that suddenly we can relate to everyone, or that we even wish to do so, or that it is wise to do so; but like all skills it increases with practice and the greater and the more powerful we become at this, that is to say the more Soulful we become, the more everyone and everything will further us. It is simply in their best interests to do so.

One might ask: but what about villains? What about thieves, rapists, serial killers and all the various perverts and dark demonic spirits that motivate or possess the less evolved person? Shouldn't we fear them? If you fear them, it is surely understandable. We have every right to protect ours'elves, our bodies, our Souls, and our Spirits. But understand that in time, as we grow in power as Spirits, these dark spirits will pose little threat to us save by way of temptation. They will not be able to harm our bodies, and it is only in so much as we may find their darkness attractive in our own s'elves that they will pose any danger to us. That day may be a long way off for most of us, but it will come. It will not be we who live in fear of them, but they truly who will live in fear of the Light and Power that is our evolved Spirit. And they will scurry from it.

In the meantime, we are well advised to make ours'elves strong in every way we can and to develop our Spirits and our Souls in all that we do. Always, in all things and all ways, we seek to improve ours'elves. This is the way to Power and Mastery. And when we seek that above all, when true Mastery over our beings becomes our deepest hunger and desire, linked with an understanding of karma, which is to say Cause and Effect, pursuing our s'elf interest becomes united with the welfare of our others, and the Way becomes easy, and all things further us.

Giving the Body Its Due

Just as it is wise, and most easy, to accumulate energy by pursuing our own attractions and interests, so it is wisest to guide the lower aspects of our being and our body by giving it what it wants in a positive fashion. This is Nature's Way. Nature wishes us to procreate, so it makes sex pleasurable. So, too, do we guide the body and our lower desires by giving them what they want in a pleasurable but also uplifting way. We would be unwise to let them control us and be mere reactionary forces, for then we become controlled by outside powers when it is s'elf control and mastery we are seeking. But the body has its needs as well and when these are fulfilled in a rewarding fashion it more readily cooperates with us.

What do we mean a rewarding fashion? The body wants nourishment. However, it can become addicted to substances, such as sweets, which when overly consumed can be destructive to the body. Thus the body needs to be feed in a healthy fashion, given the sweets it desires in a moderate and healthy quantity. Then the body will respond to us and cooperate with us ... mostly, by being healthy but also by being satisfied.

The same is true of our psyche and its desires. When these are fulfilled in a rewarding and healthy way our psyche cooperates with us and becomes an effective vehicle for the realization of our Elfin Spirit.

So, also, in nurturing those under our care we need to take note of, and attempt to fulfill all of their needs and their desires in a positive, that is healthy and Soulful fashion, so their Spirit is furthered, and they are encouraged to gain ever greater power and mastery over their own s'elves.

In rising through the planes as Elven Spirits, in living the Elven Way, we neglect no aspect of our being, nor any beings that are related to us. In this way we make progress without resistance, and without creating negative karma that would evolve into hindrances and obstructions in the future. The greater we become as Elven Spirits, the greater our responsibility to take care of all in our realm. The greater we become as Elven Spirits, the more we tend to attract those who seek what our Spirit offers; the greater we become as Elven Souls, the more we nurture those who seek us with sincerity and this nurturing ennobles us. We become royalty. We become Shining Ones.

Pursue Excellence

The Elven Way is the path of excellence. We strive to do our best, become our best in all things. This striving toward excellence becomes a habit of our being and thus becomes a permanent part of our Spirit. In striving for excellence in all things, we improve ours'elves in all we do in every way.

However, striving for excellence is not to be confused with an Obsessive-Compulsive need to have everything seem perfect. We do our best and having done so leave it at that. What we do may not always be perfect but if it is best we can do at that time it will nearly always be good enough. Remember, it is not the transitory that is seeking perfection, but the permanent, the eternal. We seek excellence not because we need every detail to be perfect but because we seek to develop that habit, that energy of doing our best in all we do. What we are perfecting is not so much a particular book, painting or other work, but our skill and ability in doing it.

We _are_ the art that we are creating. We are the masterpiece we ever strive toward. And the more we become perfectly ours'elves the closer we are to Elfin. The king and the land are one. The elf and Elfin are one.

The Elven Way is quite simple while being tremendously varied. Seek excellence in all you do, improve yours'elf in every way, nurture your others as best you can, and trust your s'elf, your interests and attractions. As long as you do not bring harm to yours'elf or others you are free to pursue your path as you see fit, and only you can decide in the long run what is right for you. And only by making that decision do you become a free elfin Spirit.

More Old Elven Sayings:

> *We elfin tend to laud self sacrifice much less than some folk*
> *but practice it more.*
> *—Elven Knowledge*

> *Those who do wrong intentionally are wicked,*
> *those who do it accidentally are foolish.*
> *Folly can learn although it doesn't always realize it needs to do so.*
> *The wicked can change but it seldom desires to do so.*
> *—Old Elven Wisdom*

> *Jesus saves, Buddha recycles, the elves dumpster dive.*

> *Most people say shit happens. The Elves exclaim, free fertilizer!*
> —Old Elven Saying

> *Most people believe the witching hour is at midnight,*
> *but the elves say the witching hour is whenever we do our magic,*
> *therefore, it may be at any hour that*
> *starlight rains down in the corner of your eye.*

> *Elves consider trees to be some of our very best friends.*

> *Elves sometimes say that trees are merely elves that grow leaves.*

> *Elven magic knows no age. It is ancient and ever young,*
> *reaching across time and transforming all it touches.*
> —Old Elven Wisdom

> *Every step toward Elfin brings us closer to our true s'elves.*
> *Every movement toward our true s'elves brings us closer to Elfin.*
> —Elven Knowledge

> Men seek peace within, elves seek Elfin.

> The Path to Elfin isn't out your door, necessarily, but through your soul.

> Elves sometimes feel an almost irrepressible urge to retreat from the needless conflict of the world and go hide together in the woods.

> The feeling you get when you draw closer to Elfin is that somehow inexplicably everything's going to turn out fine.

> Elfin is only as close as we allow it to be and never farther than our yearning for it.

> Every elf is sui generis, individual, eccentric and unique, singularities who could, each and everyone of us, spawn a whole new species of elfin being.

Section Three:

Ancient Futures

> "THE DREAM WORLD AND WHAT MOST PEOPLE CALL REALITY ARE ONE AND THE SAME TO THE ELVES, JUST DIFFERENT PARTS OF ONE REALITY, WHICH IS IN ITS'ELF A DREAM. IT IS IN THIS WAY THAT WE HAVE THE POWER TO MAKE DREAMS BECOME REAL."
> —THE SILVER ELVES

ANCIENT FUTURE

The Future exists within us as potentiality. It has always existed within us from the very beginning that always is, and will continue to its realization that always will be. Thus elves ever feel connected to an ancient past that is really our potential future. We are making actual our potential. The potential is Ancient, the actualization becomes, and thus is in what seems to be the future, although in fact it has always, and will always, exist Now. As we harmonize with this potential, make it real in our conscious being, we give it substance, and the Ancient Future becomes the Eternal Now.

The Seven Pointed Star

The Seven Pointed Star, which in its acute form is called by us the Elf Star and by the faeries the Faery Star, is a great symbol of the Elven People and represents many things to us, including but not exclusive to our association with the Seven Sisters of the Pleiades, the seven root races of humanity with their seven sub-races, the seven chakras, and the seven rays of manifestation.

It is also representative of the seven magical achievements that elevate us toward the realm of the Shining Ones that we call Elfin Faerie, which is to say these achievements illuminate our beings with light.

1. The Presence:

The Sense of the Presence is a realization of the Eternal within one's s'elf. While our current form is transitory, the energy that composes it is Eternal, and within this energy and attached to it is our Potential S'elf, the Illuminated Shining One that exists in potential and that we are in the process of shaping and bringing into realization. We actualize it. As we become increasingly aware of our true s'elf, we become ever closer to Elfin, and our own Shining Nature. Sensing this presence within us, which is sensing our true nature and its eternal aspect, is a key achievement of the path.

At first, this Presence appears as being outside of us. We sense Elfin and the supra-dimensional realms as being separate from us, calling to us from afar; but in time we realize it is in fact our own s'elves calling to us. The Call comes from within and it comes from our future s'elves, who are ever existent within us, and ever striving toward realization. Again, at first this Presence within may seem separate from us but what it wants and what we want are really one and the same, and we come in time to realize, in fact, that we *are* really one and the same. When we remove all that is illusionary from our being, we are left with our own true s'elf; and that s'elf is the Eternal Presence that is ever a part of us, and ever us.

At times this Presence manifests in the form of fantasies and imagination concerning our potential. There is no harm in this, however, it is important that we are able to distinguish the differences between our fantasies about ours'elves, and the reality of our current level of development. Many when they are young elves spend a great deal of time in the fantasy, usually as a means of escaping reality, and proclaim far and wide their titles, powers and abilities, which are theirs in potential, but not as yet actualized. At some point one steps beyond this stage and begins the real work of making the potential real. This is a long process and requires great perseverance and many give up when they realize how very long the Quest is, and how very much effort it requires. In time, however, one realizes that no matter how long it takes one will never get there if one doesn't begin and continue on persistently. This first step, while seemingly small, is really a huge leap forward.

2. Focus:

The second achievement is focus. Gradually, with continued practice we attain the ability to concentrate our will and put all our energy toward the achievement of the Great Work, which is the realization and elevation of our true s'elves. But focus is not simply a matter of concentration; it is also the narrowing of our activities. By ridding ours'elves of all that is superfluous to our goal, we direct all our energy toward the Great Quest, which is mastery over our true natures and the fulfillment of our s'elves as Soulful Spirits.

There are those who will try to achieve this in a single blow or great effort of will power. They will decide to concentrate all their energy toward the goal, and if they are able to do so and persist in this then they are already advanced adepts who have made great progress in previous life cycles. However, for most of us, gaining this achievement, just like any other thing we desire to master, will take time and practice. Know again that the harder you try to force it, the greater will be the reaction when you run out of force. Thus, gradual and continual persistent practice is best. And remember, most of us in due time require recreation. Things that divert us from the goal, harmless amusements, can be actually quite helpful if they revitalize us. Don't turn yours'elf into a fanatic. Elves and fanatics seldom willingly share the same dimensions. We tend to think them boorish and potentially, or actually, insane, and they usually view us as frivolous and simply not dedicated enough to whatever cause, god or goal they espouse.

Apply yours'elf toward your elven goals as much as you can each day and let it become a habit of being. Make it easy. Make it enjoyable. Do it because you truly wish to do it, for that is the path to the true s'elf. Find your magic, your creative outlet, for that is the path to the true elf within you. Remember, everything you do well, everything you do with excellence, is magic.

3. Calm Composure:

The more confident you become in your elven nature, the less you will tend to react to any that assail your nature or challenge your right to be who you really are, which is who you chose to be. The more you come to realize your eternal elfin nature, the less the world will distress you, and the more easily and naturally will you deal with difficulties and obstructions that arise. And these obstacles will arise on this plane of being, even when we've cleared our karma, because there are many, numerous, nearly innumerable magics, that is personal wills, seeking to fulfill thems'elves. Remember, the magic carpet is created through cross weaving the weft and warp of individual magics that are individual wills.

The more attuned we are to our true s'elves, the more calm and composed we become, the less we resist the inevitable flux of life, which is the magic being woven. We look at the world and we understand obstructions in the same way we view traffic lights. We content ours'elves with waiting, or taking the detour, and we do it all with ease. The easier we become, the easier it all becomes. The easier we take it, the easier we make it. All things become clay for our creation. Nothing and no one is neglected. Nothing is wasted. All things lead to the goal, which is the realization of our Spirit and thus the achievement of Mastery and Power.

Naturally, this takes a bit of doing. Even when most of us think we have attained mastery, something will occur to challenge that mastery, which may frustrate us. The more we can respond without frustration, the greater our mastery becomes. But the frustrating thing is, we still get frustrated at times. Forget the goal, Beloved, in as much as possible enjoy the journey and take all you can in your stride, and for the rest, keep trying, but not so hard. We have forever after all.

4. Inner Understanding:

First, we must come to understand our s'elves, our needs, our desires, our aspirations, weaknesses, tendencies, skills, abilities, proclivities and all else about our nature both transitory and eternal. From this we are wise to extend this understanding soulfully outward, so we understand others.

In saying this, however, we don't mean merely understanding them as certain psychologists might, by analyzing them and assigning them to this or that diagnosis or social category. What we mean is that we strive to understand others as they understand their own s'elves. There is the old saying of don't judge someone until you've walked a mile in their shoes, and this is of that nature. If we don't understand people from their own point of view, see them as they view thems'elves and the world, we never truly understand them at all. This inner understanding is the same as knowing the individual's True Name. If we understand them from within, we gain the ability to influence them.

This understanding also extends to all things. If we wish to use a hammer or a screw driver, or a paint brush, it helps to understand how it is best used, which does not mean we can't try to use a screwdriver as a hammer, but it's not very effective to do so. However, sometimes a screwdriver may serve as a type of palette knife for painting. This is all to say we need to know our tools to master them; we need to understand the techniques of our art to master them, even if we are to create new art forms. For each thing and each person we need to understand its current place and its potential, its strengths and its weaknesses.

Seek to understand all things from their own point of view, and the Universe will unfold its secrets unto you.

5. Openness:

It is important to become Soulfully open. This manifests in meditation as a quiet, thus open mind. It is difficult to hear if we spend all our time talking. It is through this openness or receptivity that we hear the Call. It is this openness, or awareness, by which we receive sensory data from all about us, including the parallel dimensions.

In its higher, or advanced, aspects this openness becomes intuition and psychic power of various sorts: clairaudience, clairvoyance, and much else, including direct perception of the hints and communications of the Shining Ones. It is easy to see that this achievement works in concert with, and arises from the previous achievement of Inner Understanding. It is through the power of this openness that we receive and add to ours'elves all those things that might be thought of as secret knowledge that aid us on our path and help us in our endeavor to illuminate our being and gain access to the supra-dimensional realms of being. And it is important to remember that it is only by being open to others, that is by being open to influence ours'elves, that we have any hope of influencing them.

6. Appreciation

In a certain sense, we are speaking here of a positive outlook or positive thinking, the *glass is half full* point of view combined with a *thankfulness for all our blessings* energy that is a true magic, and helps one to obtain those things one desires and that one puts energy toward. Such an outlook is truly beneficial and of great value.

But more than that we are speaking here of appreciating others. Not only expressing admiration for those who have done great things, created the books, movies, music, art that we love, or who have other great accomplishments, but also appreciating the positive in every person and by appreciating it, encouraging and nurturing it. This includes always giving credit where credit is due, including the idea of giving the Devil his due, which means appreciating the good in all beings, and acknowledging their true accomplishments even if we don't like them as people, or even if they have done terrible things as well as beneficial things. We need to ever encourage the positive aspects of every being.

This is no small feat and the more secure we become as Spirits, that is to say the less we seek continually to garner praise for ours'elves, the more we are able to give appreciation to others, to see their talents and to understand them as they understand thems'elves. And a bit more, it helps to see the potential in them that they often have yet to realize. And by realize we mean here not only make real in their lives, but to even comprehend in their own understanding of thems'elves.

There is a trick in this as well. By appreciating others without seeking appreciation ours'elves, we draw attention to ours'elves. This modesty will certainly be rewarded and people will be drawn to us as every creature is to the source of its nourishment. True modesty is so unusual in this world that it stands out as exceptional.

So show appreciation always, dear Ones. Appreciate all the blessings you have received, and appreciate the positive tendencies and abilities of everyone you meet. In doing so you will gain greater understanding and a Soulful connection to them while nurturing their spirit. This, of course, must be genuine appreciation. There are those who will fall for flattery, and many who seek sycophants, but every Soul, deep within its'elf, recognizes the true from the false, and only genuine and sincere appreciation is of any real or lasting value.

It is also true that there are many in the world who are skeptical of any appreciation, not only because they are skeptical of their own abilities, but also because they are ever wary of being manipulated through flattery. Again, make your appreciation genuine, they can accept it or reject it, that is up to them; but if it is genuine it will eventually penetrate their consciousness anyway, although you may be long gone when that happens. Much of what we say to others is never given true consideration until the individual is left to hirs'elf and sHe no longer has us to argue with, but absorbs our statements within, arguing with hir own s'elf about it. Appreciate what you observe without expectation and great magic will result from it. And remember, deep within they want to feel good about thems'elves, they hunger for recognition and appreciation. When that appreciation is genuine, reflective of their true s'elves, it can have momentous effect upon them.

7. Altruism

We could call this one Love, for love is at the heart of it. Or perhaps inter-relationship, for that is also what this achievement is about. Or even sharing, for that too goes to the heart of this achievement.

Altruism is often defined as a disinterested or selfless concern for the wellbeing of others, and in that sense Altruism is not quite the right word, for our interest in and aid of others is never really selfless once we come to understand our true connection to the Universe and all that is in it; and come to know that all we do to further others always profits ours'elves in some way. It cannot be otherwise. We are connected.

What we are talking about here is giving or sharing with no expectation of immediate reward. It is gaining that deeper understanding that we are related to all of life and whatever makes life better for any, profits us all. In that way, we act ever to create a better world, and it is that world into which we will be born in future lives.

It is true that there are some that we might offer aid to for whom it would seem no benefit, either to them or us, is accrued. Thus we must be aware of the energy we share, giving it to those for whom it will really make a difference and who will use it well, so it makes their lives, and through them the lives of others, better. In this way we optimize the impact and the effect of our giving. In a sense giving is never wasted, but there are power points, pressure points in the world, energy fulcrums that when used wisely have much greater effect than others. So give wisely.

Although, it is true that sometimes we may just give, as one might give to a beggar on the street, not knowing if they will use it for alcohol, drugs or food. And while it may be that our giving is wasted, we are not so knowledgeable that we always know the ramifications of our giving. The guide for these elves is not our minds, trying to figure out if the money will be used well or not, but our hearts. If we feel the call to give, we do so, trusting in our hearts and intuition and not worrying about where our gift goes or how it is used beyond our knowing. If the individual wastes our gift that is hir doing, not ours. Our part is only to uplift, as best we are able, those we encounter when we feel the call to do so, and trust that the energy of giving, the spirit of sharing, is much more important than the money or whatever it is we donate.

This achievement is not about money or material things, it is about understanding our interconnection to the all of life and acting always, in as much as we are able, to further our others. While we may not gain in financial rewards, we are ever benefited in Soulful development by helping our others, and the more we understand/feel our connectedness to Life, the more powerful we become. It is this connectedness that elevates us to the Supra-dimensional realms, the realms of Elfin/Faerie.

The Seven Great Obstructions

Just as there are seven great achievements that aid us toward the realization of our Soulful Spirits and help us to enter into the Supra-dimensional realms, the realms of Faerie/Elfin so, too, there are seven great obstructions that we must overcome to ascend into those realms. We could think of these as seven tests we must pass, or seven ring-pass-nots/knots, or seven barriers, that we need to transcend or cross or unravel. In doing so we are transformed as Soulful Spirits, refined by the process; and the chaff that prevented us from accessing Faerie falls to the wayside.

We could think of the Threshold to Faerie as a narrow doorway and the seven great obstructions as huge objects that we are carrying that prevent us from passing through that doorway. We simply cannot enter in if we carry those objects. In fact, these aspects are attached temporarily to our Spirits, and until we refine our Spirits enough to release these things, we are too "gross", that is to say not refined enough, to exist in those more subtle realms of being.

These are, of course, generalize obstructions, that is these are the seven great obstructions that face all Soulful Spirits. It is also possible, but we won't go into them here, that an individual elf might have obstructions that are due to hir particular personality, heritage, enculturation or upbringing that sHe will also have to overcome, but as these change with each Elfae, it would be too much to delineate all the possibilities here. However, it is also true that if one overcomes these seven great obstructions the other ones tend to be minor indeed and are much more easily disposed of. Most of these are in a way of personal Karma and have a geas or obligation/responsibility attached to them. One must accomplish a quest that by the accomplishment thereof will free them from this obligation. Or alternately, one must clear one's karmic slate.

In some cases, it is not a matter of ridding ones'elf of these qualities but transforming them. Fear may be transformed into courage, for instance. These may seem to be opposite and thus unattached, but as the understanding of the Tao informs us, all opposites are related, love may turn to hate or hate to love, and thus fear may be transformed to courage through action, and other weakness transmuted into strengths. It is in a sense a matter of spiritual weightlifting. The more we work on our faults or weaknesses the stronger we become as Spirits.

Alas, one of the great obstructions prior to dealing with these obstacles, what we may call an a priori obstruction, is our fear of viewing our weakness and faults at all. In our effort to improve ours'elves it is difficult and painful at times to acknowledge that we are indeed less than we'd like to be, and less developed than we'd like people to think we are. We must commit ours'elves to viewing our natures as they currently exist, as well as understanding our Vision and our destiny, and not put on airs, or otherwise pretend to be other than we truly, or currently, are. To progress we have to know the aspects of ours'elves that need to be developed and we need to do this with utter, and sometimes painful, truthfulness.

Sometimes these obstructions are really personal challenges we've undertaken. Take for instance individuals who are unhealthily overweight and yet when asked why they don't lose weight say they want to be loved for who they are, at the same time aspiring to the love of individuals who are both physically fit and beautiful. There are numerous psychological reasons why one may refuse to explore this aspect of their personality, but it is also the case that sometimes the individual wishes to develop their power of enchantment without reliance on beauty, wealth, social success or other miscellaneous aspects; instead they chose to strictly rely upon, and develop, the power of their personality, their individual Spirit, and thus their powers of enchantment. In this case the individual would be postponing their entry into the subtle planes of being in favor of the strengthening of a chosen power. Each chooses for hirs'elf, and it is wise not to judge too quickly, nor jump to conclusions in any particular case. There are often several factors at work in most cases of Spirit development.

1. False Sense of S'elf

As in the previous mentioned case where a person is unhealthily overweight and yet refuses to lose weight saying they wish to be loved for who they are, we often ascribe aspects to ours'elves that have nothing to do with our true natures at all. When such an individual says they wish to be loved for who they are, do they mean that being overweight is part of who they are? Obviously not, what they are saying is I wish to be loved despite my weight, loved for my personality and my spirit. And again, this is completely understandable, although it is a very daunting challenge to undertake. At the same time, we have, indeed, encountered those who have mastered this situation. Their Spirit truly rises above the appearance of their bodies.

But it is important to understand that while our bodies are significant, that is we have an obligation to our body and to our Spirit to take the best care of it we possibly can, our current bodies are not us, and we need to be clear that ultimately we are protean beings, shape shifters who can appear anyway we choose.

The same is true of certain aspects of personality. Some people may act like an asshole and say, "Well, that's just the way I am." This is just an excuse for not working on ones'elf and one's personality, and thus not developing one's Spirit by attaching ones'elf to aspects of being that are not really ones'elf, and that are not productive and beneficial to one's Soulful and Spiritual development. This only impedes our progress. We need to know what we truly want to be as a Spirit, and be clear about how to achieve this.

In saying this, however, it should be clear that the evolution of our Spirit and our Soulful nature, is just that. We mature, we change, and what we once thought defined us is replaced by more profound aspects of being. Still, in ascending into the dimensions of Faerie/Elfin, it is good to contemplate that most of what we ascribe to ours'elves are but passing phases, particularly when these notions of s'elfhood are attached to a particular material manifestation, or temporary aspects or quarks of personality. To understand ours'elves as Spirits, as Immortal Beings, or to understand the Immortal nature of our beings, we need to contemplate what is eternal in our natures as well as remember that the magic we do, that is our willful and intentional acts, shape our future.

Remember the way we treat ours'elves and our attitude toward ours'elves helps define our Spirit, but the way we treat others defines our Soul.

2. False Notion of the Universe

Just as our ideas concerning our own natures are ever limited, we are always so much more than any possible explanation or definition we might give or hold concerning ours'elves, so too is the Universe, the Magic that is the Source of All Things, beyond our capacity to delineate it. It is not that we should not try to understand It and Its workings, but we should, like wise scientists, always keep in mind that whatever theories we construct must be able to be expanded with greater knowledge and understanding, and that there is more, always more, that we don't as yet know. When we do know these things we will be One with the Source, or really when we are One with the Source, we will know and understand these things. Any definition of the Universe and the Magic is always partial and limited understanding. Every elf, in examining the Universe and seeking to understand it, hungers for the truth. Pat explanations of this God or that just won't do for us. It is not that we instantly disbelieve, but that we need to examine and contemplate such doctrines for ours'elves ever comparing them to our own understanding and experience, and ever seeking the light of truth in all things.

To this is added the fact that the Universe is absolutely protean. It is pure essence, pure potentiality, that can and does become everything possible. Thus the Universe is not this way, or that way, but every way, and we as Spirit, as we grow ever more powerful, become co-creators, shaping our own worlds and realities. As we become Soulfully aware these realities/creations intermingle harmoniously with other realities and thus Faerie is born. There are few elves who really wish to be alone or have only reflections of thems'elves to relate to. We love the variety, the company, the spontaneous and surprising energy that other Spirits bring into our lives and, of course, the love and sharing for which the true elven heart ever yearns.

There are writers who say that we elves do not love at all, but that is not accurate. It is true that our relationships tend to be less filled with the emotional trauma drama that most normal folk conceive to be love, but as the saying goes *still waters run deep*, and we elfin appear on the surface to be very still waters, indeed. Our love is deep and abiding. We love for eternity for we know ours'elves to be Elven Spirits and that those we love will be connected to us forever. Thus, yes, we may be sometimes cautious in entering into relationships, particularly as we grow in maturity, but our love is ever given freely and without expectation. We love for the joy of love and the wonder we experience of those we so greatly admire.

3. False Relationship

It is important as we mature as Souls to make our relationships genuine. It is true that fate throws us into contact with all sorts of people in the world, and this often creates a sort of friction that hones our Spirit. It is also true that many form relationships on the basis of ambition, seeking to know others not because they are truly attracted to them but because they feel these individuals can further their career in some way. This is not the best reason for forming relationship, but it is important in doing so that one treat the relationship with respect and not pretend to like the person to hir face while despising and deriding hir behind hir back.

It is not that some individuals don't deserve to be mocked. They really do, but it is important even in such a case to have a compassionate understanding in regard to the struggles sHe is encountering in hir life. It is wrong to merely use people without any regard to their well being, even if these individuals are users themselves. When we say wrong here, we do not mean that word morally, but to indicate that it is counter-productive to the development of our own Soulful nature to treat anyone in this way. The Path is not always easy, but we must struggle with our own tendency to discount others, or to fall into a mere reactive relationship to them, that is to say discounting them because they discount us. As difficult as it is, and this in our experience is not simple task, we must keep the spiritual development of each individual in our hearts and minds, even when such individuals have neither our own interests, nor even their own true interests in their own consciousness.

So, too, must we respect those with whom we interact. It is true that there are different levels of development in the Spirit world, just as there are different social levels in society, but the Soul ever seeks to transcend these differences with compassion and love. That does not mean one doesn't know of or acknowledge these differences, but that one doesn't use them to separate one spiritually and soulfully from others. This is a great challenge for all those on the spiritual path, to be evolved without feeling superior to others. In fact, a sense of superiority, and arrogance in particular, prevent one from the higher/more subtle realms of being.

This sense of superiority separates one from others and anything that promotes that sense of separation is contrary to the development of the Soul. As Soulful Spirits, it is important to sense our own uniqueness while appreciating the uniqueness of every other Spirit. This is a balance that is important to develop wherein we know ours'elf as an individual and yet sympathize with, or in fact know from experience, the struggle that other individuals face in developing their own Soulful Spirit.

Compassion and sympathetic understanding, however, are not the same as pity, which is just another way of looking down on someone and separating us from them. At the same time, and this is again no easy task, we must have compassion for individuals without lowering ours'elves to the level of those less evolved. We need to understand the differences between us without emphasizing those differences except in our own behavior as we forge onward in spiritual development and set an example of superior behavior without lording our superiority over others. Our refinement should be reflected indirectly rather than directly.

As you may intuit, this is an aspect that requires some thought and a lot of practice and is, at least for these elves, not easily achieved. In fact, elves in fiction generally, and in our experience this is often true for elves in reality, have been noted for a certain arrogance and a sense of superiority to normal folk. Part of this is surely a reaction to the way they have treated us over the ages, part due to a real understanding of our spiritual development as opposed to their own in many cases, but none-the-less, this is a great challenge for us, particularly for our Souls, much more than our Spirits, and must be overcome if we are to advance into the realms of power, influence and knowledge that only comes with a superior understanding of the interconnection of all Life, which is to say all Souls.

Do you seek true power in the worlds, this realm and the supra-dimensional Faerie realms? To gain this power we must understand ours'elves. To achieve our union with Life we need to know that we are related to all things, and everything that affects anyone affects our own realm.

4. False Separation of Spirit and Matter

There are some who create false dichotomies between the material world and the Divine. The material world, particularly sexual energy, is often viewed as being dirty or impure to these individuals, and they expect that those who are on a spiritual path abstain from contact with those things that these individuals believe to be impure, or unspiritual.

However, the Divine lives within the energetic nature of the material world, which arises from and is created by the Divine Magic. There is nothing essentially impure about the material world, except in that it fails at times to be instilled with, or realize, its Divine potentiality. We are here to infuse matter with Spirit and awaken its Soulful nature. There is nothing essentially impure about sex, in fact, sex in most cases is truly Divine; but sex without consideration for the Soulful and Spiritual nature of the individuals involved, that is to say sex without mutual respect, attraction and love is not so much impure as lacking in the Divine aspects that make it truly magical. When it involves force and coercion it takes on the karma laden aspects that dominance over others always incurs for those responsible.

The same is true of money, which is often also viewed as being impure, unspiritual or the source of all evil, but there is nothing in the nature of money that is impure or unspiritual. It is merely a tool that, like most tools, can be used for achieving good things or bad things. It is all in the way it is acquired and used that various karmas are attached to its association. Note, when these elves use the word impure (as opposed to the way most use it) we mean the tendency to accumulate karma that is contrary to the development of the Spirit and Soulful nature of the individual.

Unlike those who think we are here to separate ours'elves from this world, we elves have come to master the material realm of being. It is true we are sometimes at a disadvantage in this regard, in that in order to do this we have come to understand that mastery involves the infusion of the Divine, or the arousal of the Divine, in the material realm. This sometimes limits us from doing those things that are indeed impure, or opposed to Soulful realization. Those who are unaware of their Souls, or who have weak souls, seldom care about others and will do anything to obtain power and money. This gives them a temporary advantage over us, just as people who cheat in games have a temporary advantage over those who play fairly. But our long-term objective, the development of our Soulful Spirits as we master the material realm gives us advantages that these will never know. We are supported by the forces of spiritual evolution, the Shining Ones, who ever seek to guide and aid us, and of every being whose soulful nature responds to justice and fairness.

Success in the world and mastery of all kinds are essential qualities that are promoted by the forces of evolution, and it is unwise and a mistake to scorn worldly success or to think it unspiritual or impure, just as it is folly to forgo the life of the Soul and the Spirit in favor of worldly success. The world may be dirty, but that doesn't mean it is impure. Remember, what others think of as dirt we know to be stardust, and it is this stardust/faerie dust we use to manifest in this world.

Not everyone is obliged to seek success in the material world, there are sages and yogis who spend their life in meditation and/or evocation of mantric (use of mantras/chants/spells/prayer) magic, and that is their path and they have every right to pursue it. Each contributes to the success of the whole. However, those who scorn the world and hold themselves above it presenting themselves as being "holier than thou" and thinking themselves sanctified and saintly in comparison to others, are really still struggling with the previous challenge (Challenge #3) as they separate themselves from others Soulfully, and thus must forgo the incredible power that comes from that soulful connection.

Whether you choose to seek success in the world or not, seek not to look down upon those who make the other choice. Respect all true Spiritual and Soulful paths, and honor mastery in all its forms.

5. Self-Referencing

Individuals often feel they are the center of the Universe and there is truth to this. We are each the Center of the Universe, our own Universe, but this is not the same as saying the Universe centers around us. Each of us has our own point of view, and no other, without being in our shoes and experiencing what we experienced, will hold or understand that point of view. Each of us looks at the world from where we are, what we know, think and believe, and what we have experienced. This is only natural and really can't be otherwise. We always have to start from where we are at the moment.

This self-referencing, as we say, is only natural; however, we can never expand ours'elves, our knowledge and experience without being open to the new. It is the influence of new ideas and revelations that expand our consciousness and our being and we are best served by being open to the new, while being clear as much as possible about what we already know.

This requires an *expect the unexpected* attitude, although in a more scientific fashion of ever being open to new facts and data, and always integrating all we know and believe into a consistent whole. It is true that some scientists, certain of their particular theories argue with other scientists who are as certain in their opposition. Movement forward requires us to suspend doubt, just as it is helpful at times in dealing with Faerie/Elfin and magic to suspend disbelief, but at the same time we need to be ever open to new information. In fact, the suspension of disbelief is designed for this very purpose while the suspension of doubt enables us to proceed forward "as if" until we encounter greater understanding through new data and experience.

It is important as Soulful Spirits, as elves, that we understand that others also have their own point of view, their particular beliefs and experiences, and unless we understand them from the inside, that is see things as they see them, we cannot really know them and certainly shouldn't judge them. As we become more and more Soulfully developed, that is as we have ever-greater connection in a compassionate and understanding way with others, we gain a wider comprehension and experience, a vaster range of possibility and increased sources of information.

A common complaint these days seems to be that a person thinks it is *all about them*, and in fact, it is, although, it is not all about us individually but all about us collectively. It is only by increasing our Soulful connection to others, widening our field of contact with other beings, human, non-human, supra-dimensional that we come to see the Universe through other eyes, experience it through other hearts, and become ever more of what we are truly meant to be. We call this S'elf Referencing, seeing the world from an expanded viewpoint that always includes the understanding that there is more, ever more, to learn, experience and know. Every elf approaches the realms of Faerie knowing it is vast beyond our imagination, and that reality is stranger than fiction, and so are we.

Naturally, we have a sentimental attachment to the way things are, and the way we are used to them being. As the saying goes: *Be it ever so humble, there's no place like home.* Thus in trying to understanding the supra-dimensional realms, or our cousins who abide there, in endeavoring to understand Faerie/Elfin and its nature, we tend to base our notions upon what we already know, and have experienced. We tend to anthropomorphize nearly everything, including our ideas of Divinity, making our Gods into men and women much like us. But it is important to understand that in entering the Realms of Faerie we will give up much of what we thought we cherished, just as we often give up our interest in the toys we played with when we were children. They may hold a charming sentimental attachment in our memory, but they no longer hold real relevance in our lives. This transformation of view, however, is not something we have to force upon ours'elves. Our release of these things is just as natural as our interest in them in the first place; however, as we mature as Elfin Spirits (by Elfin Spirits we mean Soulfully developed Spirits) we become increasingly aware that we are entering realms where there are far less limitations and vastly more possibilities, and that we ever need to keep an open mind as well as an understanding that our path is not the only one that leads to Faerie.

6. False Fulfillment

Most people go from one desire to another, thinking that when they obtain this thing or that thing, or this and that thing, they will be at last happy and satisfied. But desires are like dishes, we are only ever finished with them temporarily. In the course of time, many folks come to the realization that material things and worldly success do not fulfill them. No matter how much they get, they still feel empty. They turn then to spiritual things, or spiritual ideas really, substituting faith and belief and quite often companionship upon the path for material desires.

There is surely nothing wrong in this. It is truly a step upward in realization. Alas, these individuals often find that those they thought were such "good" Christians, or Moslems, or whatever, turn out to be quite flawed individuals, and their "holy" men are not as holy as they were lead to believe. This often launches the individual into a crisis of faith, and the individual frequently gives up the pursuit of the spiritual and returns to the pursuit of the material, which is usually what sHe discovered hir supposed holy men were up to anyway.

In time, we come to realize several things. The first is that while there are many amazing individuals in the world, few, if any, are truly perfect, and those who present themselves as being holy are often the least of these. Second, while our companions on the path are seldom anymore advanced than we, or only a little so, they can bring a lightness to our journey, which despite their and our lack of perfection, makes the Path much more enjoyable and richer. It is true our companions may not be perfect, but the question is: are they fun to be around, do they arouse our spirit and help keep us focused on our true path? Third, while we can never find true fulfillment in material things or spiritual doctrines and dogmas, that doesn't mean that they are not useful to us. And finally, true fulfillment is found in the development of our own true s'elves, the perfection of ours'elves as Soulful Spirits, and the pursuit of our creative, magical and spiritual goals. It is in these things, which are the eternal pursuits of the Elfin Spirit that true fulfillment/happiness is to be discovered and experienced.

It is true that there are individuals that appear very self satisfied, who seem literally filled with themselves, but this is an illusion that bears its opposite within it. However, this very fact is to their benefit for it is in becoming dissatisfied with themselves, and their works, that they strive for that which is greater. The realization of the divine, the magical, the elven, is not found and kept, but to be ever sought after. It is not the masterpiece that makes the Master, it is the Master that makes the masterpiece. By ever striving toward perfection, we obtain the perfection of striving.

Remember our goal is the perfection of the individual Spirit in harmony with the Soulfilled Universe. While we, as individuals, are in many ways similar, we are not the same. Each has hir own happiness, that is to say something, or some things, that constitute hir happiness and the pursuit of which is energizing, rather than draining, to hir. In this, and in the association of our kindred, the Spirit is energized and true fulfillment realized. We could think of this as a game and say that the playing of the game is more important than the winning of the game, but alas that is too confusing since for many folks playing to win is what they really enjoy. Rather, it would be more accurate to call it a dance. It is the dance of magic, in which we enjoy the dance and create magic by doing so. When the dance is over what we have won is a good time dancing, and we look to the next dance eagerly. This is true also of the Path of the Spirit; it is a dance, a dance of love, life and magic.

7. False Ritual

When we speak of false ritual we are not speaking of Satanic rites or other such things mostly experienced and performed in movies, but which have their associative realization in life; however, we won't go into that here. When we speak of false ritual we mean ritual that no longer has effectivity for the individual, although it may have been effective at one time. When we speak of false ritual, we aren't simply speaking of magical rituals, in the sense of ceremonies, although they are certainly included, but of outmoded and obstructive habits and routines that bind the individual rather than liberating them.

This is the case with outdated dogmas, doctrines and religious taboos that no longer hold relevance in our current lives. Many folks pass on the prohibitions of the past and adhere to them, demanding others do as well, because their "god" told them to do so, not calculating that the significance of these things, and the reason for them, had long passed. So, also, we as Elfin Spirits need to be certain that our own rituals, routines and habits continue to be effective for our current level of spiritual development. Things that worked in the past may not continue to be productive for our spiritual evolution as we mature as spirits. This is, in part, why elven magic is often impromptu or improvised. We ever adapt other systems of magic to our own needs and continually transform our own magic as time and circumstances demand.

The Path of the Elfin Spirit demands that we become increasingly open, and open minded, ever more flexible and adaptable as Spirits. This is also the effect of progress in the

Elven Way. The further we advance as adepts, the more flexible we become. This is particularly important because the deeper we penetrate into Elfin/Faerie the more protean becomes the nature of that realm. Many of the limitations that we faced in the more form-oriented/material world fall away there, giving us greater power, but also presenting us with greater challenges, which can only be solved, like an Elfin Riddle, by a unique and individual perspective.

It is easy to become attached to habit and routine. We find ways that work for us and thus tend to repeat those methods that brought us success. Thus criminals tend to develop MO's as they practice their skills in crime. At the same time, while these habits of action help them to succeed, they are often also the source of their downfall. So, too, do we as Spirits tend to repeat those actions that work for us, it is only natural to do so, but we must ever be aware of improving what we do, not merely relying on the ways of the past that have worked previously, and in this way we are ever perfecting ours'elves.

And it is important to remember that while we can help each other on the Way, and in fact, the Way is usually made much easier when we have true companions, spiritual brothers and sisters to aid us, the Path is none-the-less individual. We must each advance on our own, while at the same time the advance of any one of us aids all of us. Still, it is ever we who must make the effort to pursue the Path, no other can do that for us. Thus the ways that have worked for others, the tried and true, may not work for us, or at least not without some adjustment and adaptation to our own Path, skills, and modes of being.

The Path is like medicine, in fact in many ways we could say the Path is medicine; it is healing for the Elfin Spirit. However, while some medicines will cure or prevent a particular disease in a hundred thousand people, it will also kill one in that hundred thousand. Some people will be allergic to drugs that work perfectly for others. We are not all the same. Many rituals that have worked for others will work for us, but not all. Remember always, you are a unique Spirit and need ever to trust your own instincts when following the Way. Do what works for you, but always keep in mind that you may be able to do it even better. By continually upgrading your skills, your magic, you grow ever closer to being the sort of Spirit that can endure long periods in Elfin/Faerie, growing ever more adapted to life on the supra-dimensional realms where the Shining Ones abide. It is important to remember that these dimensions are both more real, being closer to the Divine Source of the Magic, and more dream-like, for the same reason.

If the truth was easy to recognize there are some folk who'd still go about in disguise.

Elves often have dream catchers all over our homes. We save these dreams for when we need them.

The elves say you may inherit many things except for the power of your magical spirit and that you can only inherit from your own s'elf through the lifetimes.

Section Four:

The Shining Ones

"It is hard to say how long we might stay among you, for the choice is not entirely our own. We ours'elves are neither great nor important but we have come bearing gifts from the Spirits of the Stars and from the very heart of Elfin. We bring a feather shed from the wing of the Dove of Peace, and seeds descended from the sacred trees of Elfin, and a spark from the Eternal Silver Flame, which gave birth to all the Eldar folk. And while some will not accept it and others see it not, and others still will attempt to blow it out, it is a Flame Eternal and even extinguished it will awaken again from its very ashes and find a place in every heart that longs still for the beauty and magic of Faerie."

—The Silver Elves

SOULLESS OR SOULFUL?

Quite often in fiction we Elfae are presented as being creatures without Souls who live forever unless killed, and if we are killed we disappear forever. This is not the case. Everything and everyone in the Universe is soulfully endowed. It is true there are those who can dampen their soul to near non-existence, but the non-existence of the soul ultimately brings about the virtual non-existence of the Spirit. A Spirit alone may exist, but if it is not connected to anything but itself it thus, for all intents and purposes, no longer exists as far as anyone else is concerned. To totally lose one's soulful connection is to lose touch with everything. To be soulless is to be utterly alone and disconnected.

It is true that there are individuals who seem to care nothing for anyone but their own self, but it is important to remember that that self is composed of a universe of mini-selves. Remember, our bodies are not us, but energetic souls that we have attracted to us, and who share in our quest for success. Someday, every atom will realize its own Soulful potential as a Spirit.

If anything, we elves tend to be more soulfully developed, which is why we so often mourn the mass butchering of the trees, the extinction of other creatures, the pollution of the oceans and the atmosphere, and the wanton waste of life due to war, poverty and neglect that many normal folk are completely oblivious to and uncaring about. They cut down trees without a thought to lives of the trees, they kill animals for sport and the mass extinction of insects is nothing to them.

It is also this soul development that allows us to delve ever deeper into Elfin/Faerie. In a sense you could say that we develop a relationship with Faerie; without that relationship we simply cannot enter in. At the same time, Faerie is composed of, or created by, the relationships, the soulful connections, of the Elfae people to each other. Our relationships, our Soul connections, are the threads that weave the fabric of Faerie/Elfin. The more attuned we are to our others, that is to say the more Soulfully mature we are, the easier it becomes to enter into the Faerie realms. Entering Faerie requires us to be attuned to Nature, to our own nature and to greater Nature; and Nature, really, is animated by Soul.

Creators of faerie tales, both modern and old, often say that we Elfae don't feel like mankind does, we cannot love as they do. This is true in a sense, for we do not tend toward false trauma-drama passions like so many, but that does not mean we don't feel, as we've indicated previously. Our love runs deep and true, and it is this love, this Soulfulness that interlinks us and makes Faerie possible. We may not be as irrational as man tends to become at times, but we are a deeply intuitional folk, and our connections and feelings are inclined to be genuine rather than dramatized.

Further, we have a propensity to see the long range of life. The temporary and passing dramas that so engage much of humanity seldom move us as much as it does them because we recognize these dramas for the illusions they truly are. We look to the eternal, and therefore it is the eternal that stirs our feelings.

Most of what the majority of folk consider to be their own selves are but passing phenomena that do not pass with us from life to life. We don't take our bodies, or necessarily even the form of our bodies from one life to another, although it is more probable to achieve the same form than obtaining the same atoms from one life to another. We shed our ideas, although the tendency toward certain thought forms remain with us, and unless we are very advanced we leave behind our memories, although a sense of our experience remains within us, usually in our unconscious. Only our Spirits, that is our tendencies and abilities, and our Souls, our connections to others, which is also Karma, passes from one life to the next for most of us.

When we say that Karma is our connection to others, we mean that all karma comes from actions that have affected our relationship with others, thus Karma is really a Soulful event and designates our position in relationship to others and our obligations to them. The question is: have we increased our relationships through a lifetime, that is made a stronger and more genuine connection to life and others, or have we restricted our relationships, weakened them by preying upon others and isolating them from us? Those are the questions whose answers compose our karmic fate.

All progress is made through life. We might think of a particular lifetime as a course of study, which has many tests in it and usually at the end a very large test, a final so to speak. When we die we discovered if we have passed the course and graduated to a new and more advanced course of study, or we have failed and thus have to repeat the course. For we continue to repeat a course until we master it. The time between courses, or lifetimes, is a time of integration where what we have really learned becomes a part of our Elfin Spirit, and all that we didn't learn fades from us. It is through this process that we gradually approach the Shining Ones, who are, so to speak, our teachers and professors, although like all true teachers, they are thems'elves still learning. It is just that their studies are more advanced than ours, and mostly incomprehensible to us at our current stage of development in the same way that calculus is incomprehensible to children just beginning to learn basic math.

It is our karma, our Soul connections that bring us back, life after life, to learn our lessons here. But it is also our karma, our Soulful connections that lead us eventually to progress toward the Eternal realms of Faerie. The more our relations become of an eternal nature, the more spiritual they become, the more we are drawn into that realm where dreams come true, and our beloved kindred await us always.

What constitutes relationships of an eternal nature? Those things that help develop the Elfin Spirit in a positive way toward the realization of its nature and its destiny are of the eternal. The relationships that will last are those that have helped the individual toward hir realization of hir Elfin Spirit. This will establish an eternal bond between them. As we develop our relationship with the eternal, as we become ever more eternal in our own natures, we escape the wheel of reincarnation and become eternal beings, which is to say we develop continuity of consciousness and can then remember all we have experienced through the lifetimes, as well as developing a fairly eternal form/body (although one that is amazingly protean).

It is important to understand that karma is automatic. It is not due to the arbitrary decision of some outside person who may, like a judge in a court, dispenses justice one way for those of hir race and another for those of other races, or who might be bribed by the rich, influenced by the powerful, or otherwise affected by contrary interests. Karma is exact. It is due to the consequences of our own actions, or our choice not to act. One might wonder if one can intervene in someone's karma. If say a person has a particular disease and we believe or know that this disease is due to their karma, are we doing them a favor by healing the person? Do we have the right to do so? However, the question really is, do we have the power to do so? We may alleviate a particular situation if, indeed, we have the power to do so, but that doesn't alter the person's karma. That is to say, we can cure the disease, but that doesn't mean we've cured the individual of the tendency to act in such a way as to create such karma in the first place. However, if we have the power to cure the disease, it may be the individual has cleared hir karma. If the karma was such that it couldn't be relieved, we wouldn't have the power to do so. Yet, the fact remains, while we can help the individual heal, only the individual can alter the direction of hir Spirit and hir Soul connections.

In truth, we need not concern ours'elves with some other individual's karma; we need only concern ours'elves with our own karma. Therefore, if we have the power to help others, that is truly help and uplift their Elfin Spirits, we should consider doing so, for in doing so we shape our own karma. We create our karma, our lives in everything we do. This is the magic. When all we do has the eternal aspects of Faerie/Elfin underlying it, when all we do has the awareness that we are, indeed, doing magic, we grow ever more attuned to the Source, the Magic, the Eternal, and we become ever more clearly our own true Elfin Spirits.

The Shining Ones

Just as we have advanced beyond the mere reactionary lives of most animals, so have the Shining Ones evolved beyond us. But all beings progress through the stages of evolution, and the Shining Ones were long ago, in essence if not in exact particular, where we currently are. So, too, in the course of development will we become similar to, although not exactly alike, those great and powerful beings.

We could look at them in the way that the Catholic church does using the Angelic Hierarchy of Powers, Virtues, Cherubim and Seraphim and so forth including saints, or we could see them as the Buddhists do as Buddhic Souls, Manus, Mahachohans, Bodhisattvas, and so on, or in any other religious or spiritual doctrine. It is all the same to the elves. That great elven sage Timothy Leary called them Singularities. The terminology we use is for the convenience of those to whom we communicate, what is important is that our understanding of the Universe and these beings who endeavor to uplift us, should reflect as closely as possible our understanding of the truth and nature of existence. Thus we elves, if need be, can converse with any religious folk of whose doctrines we have knowledge (or lacking knowledge we can listen, ask, and learn) and know that we are still speaking of Elfin/Faerie and the truth of reality, though we may not use those terms at all, depending upon their intelligence, open-mindedness and flexibility.

We know that the Universe is created by the Great Spirits, the Shining Ones, the Singularities. However, we also know that the essential energy of the Universe is Eternal, it cannot be created nor destroyed, but the forms it takes depends upon our own magic, our own actions, and the magic of those, the Shining Ones, to whom we are soulfully connected. We know that any particular way of viewing the Universe is just that, a way of viewing it. As elves, we try to formulate the Universe with as much magic and beauty as we can, thus we see it as Elfin/Faerie, but we know that others have their own point of view and we do not begrudge them this. We treat them and their views, or their terminology with respect, as long as they do the same. We are not obligated to respect those who don't give their respect to others; although, we respect the Soulful potential in all beings.

Despite many fairy tales that say we elves are repelled by churches, invocations of God's name, church bells, holy water etc. the truth is the elves have no conflict with most religions. We are seldom interested in them accept in an intellectual fashion, but they don't offend us, and we sometimes find their 'magical' practices interesting. We have no conflict with someone being an elf and a Christian, or Moslem or Buddhist, or anything else, and usually it is only certain sects of those religions that would have a problem with us being elves. We do, however, have a terrible time believing in complete gibberish without any facts, or even the semblance of the truth, reality, nature, rationality or logic. Some might think that a funny, even ironic statement, coming from people who call thems'elves elves, but these haven't bothered to find out, or even ask, what our basis is for doing so.

It would be unwise of us, however, to set ours'elves against others. We know that our identity is no more than beautiful clothes we've chosen to wear and that others chose to dress differently. We dress as elves, they dress as Christians, or Buddhists, or Jews, or Moslems or whatever, but it is all dress. We find our style pleasing and trust they find theirs pleasing as well. But it would be a mistake to think we are the clothes we choose to wear. We are not even our bodies. We are Elfin Spirits and as such are connected to all things/beings in the Universe. And in time, one comes to understand that all the Universe is Being.

We know that Elfin/Faerie is not a reality that exists except, as all things do, in potentiality. It is our choice to make that potentiality actual through our own lives. The ancestors of our Race, and here we mean spiritual rather than physical race, are the Shining Ones who guide us ever toward the realization of Elfin both within us and around us. These are great and powerful Spirits whose range of operation is vast compared to our own. We live in towns and cities, and at best function on a planetary level. They function on a planetary level, the solar level, the galactic level, and beyond. They are intra- and interdimensional beings, and any thoughts we have about their make up and powers are limited by our own experience and understanding. We will only truly understand them when we advance to the point where we become like them. Fortunately for us, it is not as important for us to understand them, as for them to understand us, which they do far better than we tend to understand ours'elves.

Some also call these Shining Ones the Masters of Wisdom, and that fits them as well. These elves sometimes call ours'elves the fae, the Elfae, the pixies, brownies and other manner of folk, star children, flower children and much else. These are all adequate ways of understanding us or viewing us; so, too, are the Shining Ones known by many names.

Mastery comes in many forms. One may be a master painter, a master musician, a master of horses, dogs, auto mechanics, woodworking etc. but these Masters are the Masters of Life, Light, and Love. They are Masters of Living and as such are Eternal Immortal Beings, which is to say they are individuals who have realized their Eternal Nature. They are here to help teach us how to Live. You understand? To live forever in Light, Love, and Happiness with elegance and a bit of panache.

However, when we say they are Masters, we do not mean it in the way of saying we are therefore their slaves. They are here to liberate us, not enslave us. While others seek their various Gods to look over them and protect them, the Shining Ones seek ever to teach us the magics by which we may protect ours'elves. It is their job, their will, to empower us. At the same time, it is important to understand that we live in the worlds they, for the most part, have created. They are the primary influence in our lives. We shape our lives within their worlds. In time one realizes this is a voluntary process. It happens because we have made a bond with them. They are in a sense our parents, our elder brothers and sisters, our ancient kindred. We grow up, via evolution as Elfin Spirits, in their household. However, in time it may be that we will establish our own household, our own Universe.

At some point to we come understand that we are them, that is to say, that we are indeed elves (or whatever we choose to be), we are Shining Ones. However, in saying this we are saying *who* we are in potential. We need to also understand *where* we are. While knowing that we are to become Shining Ones, we also need, in order to do this, to understand our current limitations, our karma, our faults and our foibles, where we are as Elfin Spirits now. Naturally, there are those among the young (evolutionarily) who will make ridiculous claims about being a Shining One without having made any effort at all toward the realization of that potentiality. But it doesn't change the fact that in declaring their goal, which they do in claiming to be a Shining One, that they will eventually realize that potential. What's more, and what they will soon find disconcerting, is that those Great Shining Ones, who have already realized that potential will instantly turn their eyes toward the one who would make such a unmerited claim, and set up those life events, tests, and trials that will lead them to the actualization of this declared goal. Those who have made these unwarranted claims will most likely whine about this, but they should be accepting responsibility for their own magic while thanking the Shining Ones for their kind, although often unwanted and unexpected, attentions.

It is the Masters that inspire us, enthuse us, fill us with Spirit, excite us about life and its possibilities, and empower us so we are eager and ready to continue on the Path that leads us to Faerie. Their means of doing this is most often through inner revelation, profound experiences of synchronicity that change our lives and the way we view, experience and feel about the Universe. People looking at us from the outside, who have not had this experience, will see nothing going on at all. They can't understand it. They cannot comprehend the Call of Faerie that we experience within, anymore than they can hear its Song. But for those of us who have experienced this event, it is a profound Initiation and an Awakening, and we are never the same thereafter.

The Elite

The Shining Ones are elite beings, great Elfin Spirits of profound development and power, and those who genuinely and sincerely tread the Path of the Elven and pursue the Elven Way are among them. We are, for the most part, on what we might think of as the lower levels: nursery school, kindergarten, or elementary school, but none-the-less on the Path and we are therefore elite beings as well. One might say that we are the Chosen Ones, but it would be more accurate to say we are the Ones Who Have Chosen to strive toward higher realization and initiation. We are those who have dared to do Magick.

How then can we interact with the rest of humanity knowing that we are elite beings without being arrogant pricks, bitches and assholes? To put it not so delicately. This at least is one case where the fairy tales often have it right, we elves can be arrogant beings. However, to progress as Elfin Spirits, we must master this tendency toward arrogance. How may we do this? The answer is, in part, modesty, adaptability and the soulful realization of our true natures and the natures of those with whom we interact.

The Universe functions in balance. Things may not balance out immediately, but they always balance out in time. If we are so aware of our advanced nature that we are arrogant, we will in time be laid low, for we will be either isolated from those we see ours'elves superior to, or they will drag us down in attempt to lift themselves up. Modesty functions both for the lowly and those who are elevated. Those in inferior circumstances are lifted up by modesty. Those in a superior position, who are modest rather than arrogant, create the balance needed to continue in such an elevated position for those beneath them, by being treated with respect and as equals, support this elevated position for it uplifts them as well.

By being adaptable, we are able to fit ours'elves in with nearly any circumstances, culture or people and in this way, nearly all people seek to further us, or at least, don't bother to obstruct us. We associate with them on an equal level, whatever their level may be, while offering them due respect, which works for both the high and the low, and thus they become, without realizing it, kindred to us, our accomplices and our cohorts.

By seeing the soulful nature of every Spirit, we act in such a way to further the Soul and the Spirit of everyone we encounter, thus every Spirit seeks to further us, although they are not always aware of this unconscious inclination to do so. It is a particularly elfin magic.

It is true that we cannot trust everyone, and have no need or obligation to get involved with everyone we encounter. It would neither be wise in this world, nor safe to do so. However, while we may not get involved with certain people socially or commercially, we still seek through magic and blessings to further their beings, their Spirit, and awaken their Souls. We are wise to understand that this is our world, our Elfin and we have the right to influence all we encounter toward their better natures as best and in whatever way we can.

We should note that in exerting such influence we are, in part, taking responsibility magically for these individuals. They come to belong to us, and our domain. Many might think that in saying this that we are contradicting ours'elves, for it sounds as though they become our servants, subjects or slaves. This is not the case. These individuals to whom we connect magically belong to us in the same way that our beloved belongs to us, or our children belong to us, or our heart, our hand or our foot. They are a part of us, make a greater life possible for us, easier for us, and it is wise to treat them in the very best fashion we can. They aren't our subjects, servants or slaves, although they may indeed serve us as we serve them in furthering their Elfin

Spirits, but if our magic is effective they may become our Allies, friends, kindred and lovers.

We may think of the Elven Way, the Path of Initiation, the Frasority of the Elite as a sort of pyramid scheme. The more successful those below us become, the more successful we are. Thus we do all we can to uplift our others, for in doing so we are uplifted.

It is important to understand that there are all sorts of elites in the world. There are elites of wealth, elites of power, elites of beauty, intelligence, and genius. Elves may belong to any or all of these elites, but the true elite is the elite of Soulful Spirit and this is also the way to the fulfillment of all one truly desires. Beauty may pass away with age, wealth or power may be lost, and many an individual has come to the end of their life and faced death wondering what it was all about, if their life had any meaning at all. It is this meaningfulness that attaches us to the Realms of Elfin and the Eternal. The true elite is the elite of profound meaningfulness. By touching lives in healing and empowering ways our own life takes on meaning and we step into the Eternal. Welcome home, beloved kindred. Welcome to Faerie. Its good to have you among us again.

If the path of life was always smooth we'd slip and fall.
—Old Elven Koan

"Jewels on the pommel don't necessarily make for a mighty sword."
—Olde Elven Saying

ABOUT THE AUTHORS

The Silver Elves are a family of elves who have been living and sharing the Elven Way since 1975. We are the authors of *The Book of Elven Runes: A Passage Into Faerie*; *The Magical Elven Love Letters, volume 1, 2, and 3*; *An Elfin Book of Spirits: Evoking the Beneficent Powers of Faerie*; *Caressed by an Elfin Breeze: The Poems of Zardoa Silverstar*; *Eldafaryn: True Tales of Magic from the Lives of the Silver Elves*; *Arvyndase (Silverspeech): A Short Course in the Magical Language of the Silver Elves*; *The Elven Book of Changes: A Magical Interpretation of the I Ching*; *The Elven Book of Dreams: A Magical Oracle of Faerie*; *The Book of Elven Magick: The Philosophy and Enchantments of the Seelie Elves, Volume 1 & 2*; *What An Elf Would Do: A Magical Guide to the Manners and Etiquette of the Faerie Folk*; *The Elven Tree of Life Eternal: A Magical Quest for One's True S'Elf*; *Magic Talks: On Being a Correspondence Between the Silver Elves and the Elf Queen's Daughters*; *Sorceres' Dialogues: A Further Correspondence Between the Silver Elves and the Founders of the Elf Queen's Daughters*; and *Discourses on High Sorcery: More Correspondence Between the Silver Elves and the Founders of the Elf Queen's Daughters*.

We have had various articles published in *Circle Network News Magazine* and have given out over 6,000 elven names to interested individuals in the Arvyndase language, with each elf name having a unique meaning specifically for that person. If you wish to know more about us you can read pages 100 to 107 in *Circles, Groves and Sanctuaries*, compiled by Dan and Pauline Campanelli (Llewellyn Publications, 1992), which contains an article by us and photos us and our home/sanctuary as it existed at the time. You can also find an article about us in volume 4 number3, issue # 15 of *Renaissance Magazine*. We are also mentioned numerous times in *Not In Kansas Anymore* by Christine Wicker (Harper San Francisco, 2005), and *A Field*

Guide to Otherkin by Lupa (Megalithica Books, 2007). The Silver Elves are also included in Emily Carding's book *Faery Craft*.

The Elven Way is the spiritual Path of the Elves. It is not a religion. While all elves are free to pursue whatever spiritual path they desire, or not as the case may be, these elves are magicians and follow no particular religious dogma. We do however believe in all the Gods and Goddesses, (also Santa Claus [to whom we're related], the tooth fairy [distant cousins] and the Easter or Ostara Bunny [no relation].) and try to treat them all with due respect. The Elven Way promotes the principles of Fairness, that is to say both Justice, Elegance and Equal Opportunity and Courtesy that is respectful in its interactions and attitude toward all beings, great or small. We understand the world as a magical or miraculous phenomena, and that all beings, by pursuing their own true path, will become whomever they truly desire to be. Our path is that of Love and Magic and we share our way with all sincerely interested individuals.

We welcome you to contact us through our website at: http://silverelves.angelfire.com or join us on our Facebook pages, under the name Michael J. Love (Zardoa of the SilverElves) or Martha Char Love (SilverFlame of the Silver Elves), and visit our two blogs exploring the Elven Way at https://thesilverelves.blogspot.com and at https://silverelves.wordpress.com.

IF WE CAST STARDUST ON THIS PAGE AFTER WE WRITE THIS, WILL YOU SEE IT? DO YOU?
—*THE SILVER ELVES*

Made in United States
Troutdale, OR
12/02/2023